DERBY GENEALOGY

Three hundred copies of this book have
been printed from type and the type
distributed.
This copy is number

DERBY GENEALOGY

BEING A RECORD
OF THE
DESCENDANTS OF
THOMAS DERBY
OF
STOW, MASSACHUSETTS

Viola A. Derby Bromley

HERITAGE BOOKS
2011

HERITAGE BOOKS

AN IMPRINT OF HERITAGE BOOKS, INC.

Books, CDs, and more—Worldwide

For our listing of thousands of titles see our website
at
www.HeritageBooks.com

A Facsimile Reprint
Published 2011 by
HERITAGE BOOKS, INC.
Publishing Division
100 Railroad Ave. #104
Westminster, Maryland 21157

— Publisher's Notice —
In reprints such as this, it is often not possible to remove blemishes from
the original. We feel the contents of this book warrant its reissue despite
these blemishes and hope you will agree and read it with pleasure.

International Standard Book Numbers
Paperbound: 978-0-7884-1543-2
Clothbound: 978-0-7884-8628-9

CONTENTS

ILLUSTRATIONS

PUBLISHERS' NOTE

This volume makes no attempt to trace all the Dabys, Darbys, and Derbys in America. It is limited to the descendants of Thomas Derby, of Stow, Massachusetts. The genealogy of another Derby stock has been compiled by Professor Samuel C. Derby, of Columbus, Ohio, but has never been printed. His manuscript, we believe, has been deposited in the Boston Public Library, where it may, no doubt, be consulted by those who do not find their names or those of their ancestors in the present volume. But there were still other Derbys established in America at an early date, some of whom are referred to in the Introduction, which, however, makes no attempt to be exhaustive.

The arrangement adopted in this book is simple. An individual number is given to every descendant of Thomas Derby mentioned in the book, the treatment of persons who died unmarried or in infancy not differing in this respect from that of heads of families whose descendants are traced further. This is logical and scientific, permitting further references to any persons mentioned in the work by these numbers. It permits future critics simply to say, for example, that "55, Derby Genealogy, unaccounted for; married and died at such and such a time, and had this and that child," or that "100, Derby Genealogy, did *not* die young, as has been supposed."

In certain systems such numbers are given only to those whose descendants are traced further, and are thus family and not really individual numbers. In the present work, children who become heads of families, which are noticed further on, are distinguished by the words "See Family —, page —," while each family in turn appears under the caption, "Family —, *see page —.*"

The page references are for the sake of the many who complain of difficulty in tracing out their lineages in numbered genealogies, in spite of the supposed scientific character of current standard systems and their undoubted simplicity to the initiated. In the present book the name of every child whose descendants are traced further is followed by the number of his own family

and of the page of the book on which it appears, while the caption
above each family is a reference back from the head of that family
to the page where he or she appears as a child in his or her
parents' family. Those who find difficulty with current systems
need, in the present case, only to look up in the Index the page
on which appears their own name, or that of parent or grand-
parent, as the case may be, from which point the lineage is easily
traced both up and down by means of the family numbers and
page references.

  This system has been adopted at the suggestion of The
Genealogical Department of The Grafton Press, which has also
devised the Owner's Lineage at the end of the book. By means
of this arrangement the owner of any copy of this book need
trace out his ancestral line but once, writing the name of each
ancestor in the proper space, with the ancestor's individual number,
and the pages of the volume where the ancestor's name appears.
Every feature of his personal lineage is thereafter indexed for
convenient reference.

FRANK ALLABEN,

Director Genealogical Department, The Grafton Press.

INTRODUCTION

The antecedents in England of Thomas Derby, of Stow, Massachusetts, have never been ascertained. An ancient Lincolnshire family of Darby or Derby bore arms, *argent, a chevron between three garbs, sable.*

The first notice of the Darby family which we have met with, says Thompson, in his *History and Antiquities of Boston, England,* is in a pedigree of the Tamworth family, where it is stated that Nicholas Tamworth, of Tamworth, married Jane, the daughter of —— Darby, of Leverton. This was about the year 1200. Ralph de Darby, of Bennington, occurs in 1346, Thomas in 1346 and 1353, and Robert in 1357. Roger Darby, of Leverton, married Elizabeth, daughter of Thomas Strange. Their son Ralph married Alice, daughter of John Read, of Wrangle. This Ralph Darby is mentioned by Dugdale as residing at Leake in 1517. His son, Thomas Darby, of Bennington, is mentioned in 1536, 1539, 1540 and 1544. Alicia, or Alice, his wife, daughter of John Langton, is mentioned in 1547. William, son of Thomas and Alice, was alive in 1571. His son, William Darby, was living about 1620. We find mention of Thomas Darby, of Leake, in 1597, 1602 and 1642. He died in 1659.

A Thomas Darby, of Leverton, occurs also in 1642.

There are several memorials of the Darby and Gilbert families in the floor of the chancel of the church at Leake.

At a short distance from the Moat House is a large ancient building called Darby Hall, which was the residence of the family of that name who were considerable proprietors in this and the adjourning parishes for several centuries, and allied by marriage to the Dymocke family.

Darby Hall is partly in Leake and partly in Leverton. It is now the property of the heirs of Oldfield. We do not know whether the chief branch of the Derby or Darby family resided at Bennington or at the house above mentioned, standing partly in Leake.

Ralph Darby resided in Leake in 1517, William Derby in 1571, and Thomas Derby in 1797. Another Thomas Derby died at Leake in 1659. Dymoke Darby died at Leake in 1701.

So far Thompson. Some Darbys or Derbys settled in New England at an early date. The Company of New England, says J. B. Felt in his *Annals of Salem* (1845, page 110; and vol. ii., 1849, page 526), consisting of many worthy gentlemen in the City of London, Dorchester, and other places, aiming at the glory of God, the propagation of the Gospel of Christ, the conversion of the Indians, and the enlargement of the King's dominions in America, and being authorized by His Royal letters patent for that end, at their very great costs and charges, furnished five ships to go to New England for the further settling of the English plantation that they had already begun there. To human perception, all was dark concerning the political career of this commonwealth when William Darby, of Dorchester, England, petitioned the Council for New England, February 18, 1623, that Richard Bushrode, of the same town, and his associates might begin a plantation at Cape Ann, which led to the settlement of Naumkeag, now Salem.

The original manuscripts of T. L. Winthrop, given in the Collections of the American Antiquarian Society, vol. iii., cxxxv., under the "Origin of the Company of Massachusetts Bay that came with Winthrop," contain the "Representatives to General Court in England, held at Deputyse House," October 12, 1629, as follows:

William Darby,
John Smith,
George Philips,
Simon Whitcomb,
John Davenport,
Thomas Andrews,
Theophilus Eaton,
John Endicott.

The will of Roger Harlakenden, County of Essex, England, names as one to settle his estate, Henrye Darby, "now of Newton, in the Massachusetts Bay of America."

Savage refers to John Derby, of Plymouth, Massachusetts in 1637, son of Christopher, from the west part of Dorsetshire, England. He removed to Yarmouth before 1643, when John Derbe,

Yarmouth, appears among those able to bear arms, and was dead in February, 1652. The inventory of his estate is dated February 22, 1656. He had a son, born the last day of February, 1648, whose name is lost from the record, and a son, Matthew, born February 8, 1650. Matthew was subsequently of Barnstable, and, according to the statement of one Joseph Lumbert, made to one Simon Bringley in the street, in July, 1671, Matthew Darby, of Barnstable, was to receive all of the property of one John Turner if the latter failed to return from sea. Sarah Darby, of Barnstable, who married Jabez Lombard, December 1, 1660, was probably a sister of Matthew.

Richard Derby, of Plymouth, 1637, called "gentleman," was a brother of John, of Plymouth, 1637, and thus another son of Christopher. Richard Derby sold twenty acres of land to Edward Doty in September, 1639. (*Plymouth Colony Records, vol. xii., page* 38). This Christopher and his son John were undoubtedly referred to in the will of "John Chipman, now of Barnstable, in the Government of New Plymouth in New England in America, being ye only son and heir of Mr. Thomas Chipman, late deceased at Brinspittle, about five miles from Dorchester in Dorsetshire in England," in which document he refers to "his kinsman Mr. Christopher Derby" and the latter's "son, John Derbe."

These Derbys are probably to be identified with the family of that name, of Asherswell, now called Stirthill, in Dorsetshire, England, mentioned in Hutchin's *History of Dorsetshire,* as the Derbys of Asherswell, lessees of property which was once a manor and hamlet. A Christopher Derby was buried at Asherswell in 1603, while Thomas Derby, son of another Christopher, was baptized at Stirthill, or Asherswell, in 1616. Reference is also found to Christopher Derby, gentleman, of Dorchester, in Dorsetshire, England, who flourished at a period which would suit the identification of him with the Christopher, father of John and Richard, of Plymouth, Massachusetts.

Agnes Derby, relict of Augustine Derby, of Bisley, in the County of Surrey, England, made a nuncupative will May 20, 1650, proved June 1, 1650, in which she bequeathed a sum in trust to Henry Collier, of Horsabell, yeoman, "He to pay Edward Derby, in New England, ten pounds when he shall come and demand the same."

This Edward Derby was of Braintree, Mass., and may be identical with the Edward Darby who, according to the *Boston Records*, was married to Susanna Hook, January 25, 1659, by Richard Bellingham, Deputy Governor. The latter settled in Weymouth, Massachusetts, where, according to the *Weymouth Records*, he had a daughter Mary, born December 29, 1660, and Priscilla, born June 20, 1672. Probably he was the father of Edward Derby who married first, in Weymouth, about 1687, Ruth, daughter of Simon Whitmarsh, by whom he had a son, Edward S. Derby, born in Weymouth, May 18, 1688; and who married, secondly, in 1705, Rebecca (Sumner) Hobart, of Hingham, Mass., who was born at Lancaster, the daughter of Roger and Mary Josselyn Sumner, of Milton.

Joseph and Thomas Daby, Darby or Derby, who removed from Concord to Stow, are supposed to have been brothers, but documentary proof of such a relationship has not been found. Nor is it known whether they or either of them belong to the Derby family of Plymouth, that of Braintree, or that of Weymouth, Mass., or whether they were immigrants, born in England.

Of these two, Cornet Joseph Daby married at Sudbury, Mass., January 14, 1676-77, Jane Plympton, daughter of Thomas and Abigail (Noyes) Plympton. She was born August 18, 1655, and died at Stow, Mass., March 7, 1728. Joseph Daby married, secondly, Elizabeth (Flagg) Clark in Concord, about 1731. She was a daughter of Eleazer Flagg and Debora Barnes, and married, first, Benjamin Clark and, secondly, Joseph Daby. She died October 21, 1784, aged 93 years.

The pages which follow are devoted to Thomas Derby and his descendants.

Acknowledgment is here made of a special indebtedness to Miss Mary L. Derby, daughter of Benjamin Derby of Leominster, Massachusetts, for her valuable assistance in connection with this work; and to her and to the many others who have furnished information the compiler expresses her thanks.

V. A. B.

FIRST GENERATION

FIRST GENERATION

FAMILY 1.

1. Thomas¹ Derby, Darby, or **Daby,** in 1684 removed from Concord, Mass., to Stow, Mass., with his wife **Mary.** Stow was incorporated May 16, 1683, at which time "12 foundation lots," each containing 50 acres of upland and 15 of meadow, were granted to the first settlers in the following order: Rev. Boaz Brown, Gershom Heald, John Butterick, Ephraim Hildreth, Thomas Stevens, Stephen Hall, Samuel Buttrick, Joseph Freeman, Joseph Darby, Thomas Gates, and Shadrack Hapgood. Other lots were afterwards granted, including one to Thomas Darby on June 17, 1684. Thomas and Joseph Darby, or Daby, as their names were often written, were from Concord (Shattuck's *History of Concord,* pages 44-45). Thomas Daby was a Narragansett soldier under Capt. Joseph Sill in King Philip's War, 1676; and may have been the Thomas Daby who joined the First Church of Salem, Mass., October 5, 1863. Thomas Daby of Stow was elected in 1706, a deacon of the Stow Church, which was organized in 1706. He died before December 29, 1749. His wife Mary died January 4, 1727, at Stow.

Children, born in Stow:

2   i. Elizabeth, baptized November 2, 1684.
3   ii. Mary, baptized July 26, 1685, died May 10, 1765.
4   iii. John, born January 26, 1687. Family 2, page 19.
5   iv. Esther, born October 19, 1690.
6   v. Joseph.
7   vi. Robert, died December 6, 1759. Family 3, page 20.
8   vii. William, married in Canterbury, Mass., June 9, 1718, Elizabeth Spaulding, daughter of Ensign Edward Spaulding.

SECOND GENERATION

SECOND GENERATION

FAMILY 2.

See page 15.

4. John Daby (*Thomas*[1]), born January 26, 1687, married, first, **Hannah**, who died November 17, 1744, aged 58 years 5 months, and married, secondly, widow **Elizabeth Holden** of Groton, Mass., April 20, 1747. She was born in 1689, and died September 9, 1767.

John Daby was one of the original petitioners for the creation of the town of Harvard in 1731. His estate was partly within the old Lancaster bounds. He bought of John Willard, October 27, 1718, lands lying upon both sides of the brook at the northern end of Pine Hill, extending along the Lancaster and Stow Line. He was a blacksmith, and his son, Joseph, a joiner. Together they built a saw and grist mill or mills upon the stream at the western foot of Pine Hill about the date of Harvard's incorporation. Joseph Daby is mentioned as proprietor of a gristmill in 1748. He sold both cornmill and sawmill to Jonathan Symonds in 1751. John Daby's sawmill is mentioned in the records as early as 1733, when he provided a part of the material for the meeting-house. From the first he held a prominent place in town, his pew in church being the third in dignity. The site of his first home is not definitely known, but appears to have been in Stow Leg, near the Lancaster line. John Daby was Corporal in 1757 (Nourse: *History of Harvard*). The following items appear in the records: "Feb. ye 3rd, 1723-4, John Darby for Som alowance for a hiway Taken Through ye Land he purchased of John Willard.

"We also mesored the Hiway in John Darbes Land and find it to Run in his Land one hundred and fifty Rods and we think he ought to be alowed three acres for one, this return was exsapted the hiways alowed and ye alowances Granted by the Propriety." (*Annals of Lancaster,* page 210.) John Daby died January 6, 1769, in Harvard, Mass.

Children:

9   i. Nahum, born February 23, 1712, in Concord. Family 4, page 23.

10   ii. Simon, born February 27, 1714, in Stow. Family 5, page 23.

11   iii. Joseph, born December 15, 1716, in Stow. Family 6, page 24.

12   iv. Hannah, born January 20, 1720, in Stow; married William Whitcomb.

13   v. Mary, born October 24, 1722, in Stow; married, first, Gates; secondly, Wheeler.

14   vi. Robert, born October 24, 1722, in Stow. Family 7, page 25.

15   vii. John, Jr., born about 1740. Family 8, page 25.

16   viii. Thomas.

FAMILY 3.

See page 15.

7. **Robert[2] Daby** (*Thomas[1]*), married **Martha**, and died December 6, 1759, an aged man. In August, 1724, the Selectmen of Lancaster entered their caution against Robert Darby who, with others, had been warned to depart said town as per their caution on file (*Annals of Lancaster*).

Children, born in Concord (Boston Records):

17   i. Anna, born November 11, 1706.

18   ii. Thomas, born November 20, 1709.

19   iii. Martha, born January 14, 1711.

20   iv. John, born May 4, 1715. Family 9, page 26.

21   v. Robert, born December 20, 1717.

THIRD GENERATION

THIRD GENERATION
FAMILY 4.
See page 20.

9. Nahum[3] **Daby** (*John,*[2] *Thomas*[1]), born February 23, 1712; married, first, **Hannah,** and, secondly, **Mary.** He was a cordwainer, and lived in Harvard, Mass. He died March 12, 1770.

Children:

22   i. Nahum, born September 2, 1743; married Susanna Worster, daughter of Ebenezer and Mary Worster, of Harvard, October 18, 1768.

23   ii. Mary. Family 10, page 26.

24   iii. Eunice, born February 27, 1746-7; died February 23, 1769 (*Harvard Records*).

25   iv. Hepsibeth, born December 2, 1748; died April 16, 1769.

26   v. William, born July 26, 1751; a soldier in War of Revolution, from Ashby.

27   vi. Jonathan, born March 13, 1753; a soldier in War of Revolution, from Ashby.

28   vii. John, born April 30, 1755.

29   viii. Salmon, born September 9, 1757.

30   ix. Daniel Sawyer, born March 30, 1760; married Abigail Sawyer, February 17, 1784.

31   x. Amos, born April 27, 1762; a soldier in War of Revolution, from Acton.

FAMILY 5.
See page 20.

10. Simon[3] **Daby** (*John,*[2] *Thomas*[1]), born February 27, 1714, in Stow; married, first, **Mercy Willson,** daughter of John **Willson,** of Andover, Mass. She was born August 21, 1717, and died August 31, 1751, at Groton, Mass. He married, secondly, **Esther Foster,** daughter of Andrew and Mary (*Smith*) **Foster,** of Andover, Mass. She was born February 1, 1734, and died October 18, 1769, in Harvard, Mass. He married, thirdly, **Judith,** widow of Jonathan **Symonds** of Harvard, July 29, 1770. Simon Daby

was appointed one of the Church Committee December 30, 1774.
Children, born in Harvard, by first wife:

32   i. Thomas, born September 22, 1739. Family 11, page 29.
33   ii. John, born March 24, 1741; married Dinah Willard,
          September 30, 1766, in Harvard.
34   iii. Mercy, born September 24, 1742; married Ambrose
          Hale, July 25, 1768, in Harvard.
35   iv. Hannah, born November 21, 1746; married Ebenezer
          Gilson of Pepperill.
36   v. Phebe, born in 1848; died in 1759 (*History of Groton*).
37   vi. Sarah, born August 31, 1751; died September 20, 1751
          (*History of Groton*).
    By second wife:
38 vii. Phebe, died an infant.
    By third wife:
39 viii. Lucy, born February 2, 1772.
40   ix. Calvin, born July 4, 1773; died July 30, 1773.
41   x. Calvin, born August 26, 1775.

FAMILY 6.

See page 20.

11. Joseph³ Daby (*John,² Thomas¹*), born December 15, 1716;
married, first, **Elizabeth Nourse**, June 8, 1738, a daughter of
Benjamin **Nourse** of Framingham, Mass., and of his wife Eliza-
abeth (*Sautel*) **Morse**, widow of Joseph Morse of Watertown, Mass.
He married, secondly, **Elizabeth Wheelock**, May 11, 1761, in
Leominster, Mass. They were married by Rev. John Rogers.
Elizabeth Wheelock was a daughter of Jonathan and Elizabeth
Wheelock. She died December 24, 1803, age 89 years. Joseph
Daby died September 7, 1792, in Leominster. He was a wheel-
wright and joiner.

Children, born in Leominster, by first wife:
42   i. Elizabeth, born October 16, 1738; married Simeon
          Perry, November 9, 1766.
43   ii. Esther, born July 17, 1740; married Cornelius Lawler,
          October 4, 1764.
44   iii. Joseph, born in 1745. Family 12, page 29.
45   iv. Benjamin, born September 24, 1747. Family 13,
          page 30.

46　v. Deliverance, born December 27, 1748.　Family 14, page 30.

47　vi. Joshua, born October 17, 1751.

48　vii. Simon, born in October, 1753.　Family 15, page 31.

49　viii. Mary.

Joseph, Joseph, Jr., and Deliverance Daby, of Derby, were soldiers in the Revolution (*Massachusetts Records*). Benjamin Nourse was Selectman, 1702, and died in Framingham. His will was proved February 13, 1748. The family of Nurse is noticed as in Sussex, Eng. Sir D. Nurse, born in the 17th century, was of Chitingstone, in that county. (*Berry's Genealogies of the County of Kent*). Barry, (*History of Framingham*, page 102) gives the following: "The town directed the seating of the meeting-house according to each one's proportion of all the taxes assessed for the meeting-house; that those arriving at sixty years of age, should be added 4d. per year to each one's rates; and that the seats be dignified as in the old meeting-house, till they come to the fifth seat below; and the rest to fall in successively. May 22, 1738, voted that Mr. Benj. Nurse be seated in the deacons' seats."

FAMILY 7.

See page 20.

14. Robert³ Derby (*John,² Thomas¹*), born October 24, 1722; married **Hannah Farren**, March 17, 1757. They were married by Justice Minot in Concord, Mass. He married, secondly, **Hannah Haywood**, November 16, 1768, the marriage being performed by Rev. Mr. Bliss (*Concord Records*). He married, thirdly, **Lucy**. Robert Derby died October 15, 1804, aged 82 years. Lucy, his wife, died October 27, 1810, aged 80 years (*Church Records*).

FAMILY 8.

See page 20.

15. John³ Daby (*John,² Thomas¹*), born about 1740, married **Sarah Hapgood**, October 21, 1764, in Harvard, Mass. She was born June 16, 1744. He was in the French and Indian War, and served at Lake George. He died October 10, 1799.

Children:

50　i. Simon, born May 20, 1765; married Joanna Hale, June 1, 1788, in Harvard.

51   ii. Asa, born February 6, 1767. Family 16, page 31.

52   iii. Mercy, born May 11, 1769.

53   iv. Sarah, born February 7, 1772; married Josiah Stone, September 13, 1797.

54   v. Betsey, born May 7, 1774; married Joshua Philips, June 26, 1800, in Fitchburg.

55   vi. John, born January 9, 1779.

FAMILY 9.

See page 20.

20. John³ Daby (*Robert,² Thomas¹*), born May 4, 1715; married **Susanna,** who died June 14, 1773. He died June 12, 1777 (Harvard Records).

Children (Boston, Middlesex County, Record):

56   i. John, a twin, born April 11, 1735.

57   ii. Rebecca, a twin, born April 11, 1735.

58   iii. Lucy, born May 4, 1739, in Concord.

59   iv. Anne, born October 16, 1741, in Concord; married John Colburn.

60   v. Elisabeth, born January 2, 1743, in Concord.

61   vi. Nathaniel, born August 23, 1746, in Concord. In Revolutionary War.

FAMILY 10.

See page 23.

23. Mary⁴ Daby (*Nahum,³ John,² Thomas¹*), married **James Joslin,** January 8, 1767, in Leominster. He was a son of John and Lucy (*Wilder*) **Joslin,** and was born July 31, 1747. They removed to Ashburnham, Mass.

Children:

62   i. James, baptized in Ashburnham, October 11, 1770.

63   ii. Molly, baptized in Ashburnham, —; married William Burrage.

There were other children, of whom we have no record.

FOURTH GENERATION

FOURTH GENERATION

FAMILY 11.

See page 24.

32. Thomas[4] **Derby** (*Simon,*[3] *John,*[2] *Thomas*[1]), born September 22, 1739; married **Mary Holt,** September 6, 1764, in Harvard, Mass. They were married by Rev. Joseph Wheeler, and removed in 1771 to Chesterfield, N. H.

Children:

64　　i. Lydia, born October 30, 1776.
65　 ii. Asa, born January 16, 1782.
66　iii. Oliver.
67　 iv. Elnathan.
68　　v. John, married Lucy Chaffin of Acton, June 22, 1784.
69　 vi. Molly, born May 10, 1765 (*Harvard Records*).

FAMILY 12.

See page 24.

44. Joseph[4] **Darby** (*Joseph,*[3] *John,*[2] *Thomas*[1]), born in 1745; married **Abigail Bennett,** April 22, 1766, in Leominster, Mass. They were married by Rev. John Rogers. Abigail was a daughter of Nathan and Abigail **Bennett,** and was born March 30, 1748. She died May 16, 1824. Joseph Darby died September 13, 1825. They lived and died in Leominster.

Children, born in Leominster:

70　　i. Nathan, born August 4, 1766. Family 17, page 35.
71　 ii. Betty, born May 4, 1769; married to Elias Dannels, May 20, 1798, by Rev. F. Gardner.
72　iii. Joseph, born March 31, 1771.
73　 iv. Abigail, born June 14, 1775; married to William Buckley, March 26, 1803, by Rev. F. Gardner.
74　　v. Joshua, born March 9, 1777. Family 18, page 35.
75　 vi. John, born in 1781. Family 19, page 36.
76　vii. Damaris. Family 20, page 36.

FAMILY 13.

See page 24.

45. **Benjamin**[4] **Daby** (*Joseph,*[3] *John,*[2] *Thomas*[1]), born September 24, 1747; married, first, November 6, 1770, a wife who died in childbirth. He married, secondly, **Rebecca Hart** of Lunenburg, December 11, 1774. They were married by Edward Hartwell, Esq., Justice of the Peace. Rebecca was a daughter of Thomas **Hart** of Lynnfield, and of Phebe (*Eaton*) **Hart** of Reading, Mass. Benjamin Daby was a wheelwright, and died at Leominster, January 15, 1817. His second wife, Rebecca, was born in Reading, March 17, 1754, and died in Leominster, January 18, 1827.

Children, born in Leominster:

79   i. Benjamin, born in 1775. Family 21, page 37.
80   ii. Phebe, born in 1778; died April 21, 1853; unmarried.
81   iii. Joseph Hartwell, born February 22, 1780. Family 22, page 37.
82   iv. Thomas, born April 19, 1782. Family 23, page 38.
83   v. Lucinda, born in 1789. Family 24, page 38.
84   vi. Fannie, born June 28, 1793. Family 25, page 38.
85   vii. Rebecca, born in May, 1797. Family 26, page 39.
86   viii. Reuben, died February 19, 1830; unmarried.

FAMILY 14.

See page 25.

46. **Deliverance**[4] **Daby** (*Joseph,*[3] *John,*[2] *Thomas*[1]), born December 27, 1748; married, first, **Mrs. Rheuamah Brown**, March 2, 1773. He married, secondly, a wife who died January 27, 1823. He was a Revolutionary soldier (*Massachusetts Records*), and died December 13, 1823. All of the family are buried in Leominster.

Children, by first wife:

86a   i. A child who died young, January 3, 1799. On her tombstone we find the following lines:

> When Christ ascends His humble throne
>   And bids the world appear,
> Thrones are prepared for all His friends
>   Who humbly love Him here.

FAMILY 15.

See page 25.

48. **Simon⁴ Daby** (*Joseph,³ John,² Thomas¹*), born October, 1753; married **Sarah Knight**, April 14, 1778; both of Leominster. He died April 14, 1812. She died November 29, 1821. Sarah was noted for her beauty.

Children:

87   i. Simon, born April 22, 1779. Family 27, page 39.
88   ii. Sarah, born August 15, 1781. Family 28, page 40.

FAMILY 16.

See page 26.

51. **Asa⁴ Daby** (*John,³ John,² Thomas¹*), born February 6, 1767; married **Elizabeth Houghton**, July 3, 1796. She was a daughter of Rufus **Houghton** of Leominster, who was in the Lexington Alarm, 1775. We find the name of Asa Daby as Ensign, March 23, 1795 (*History of Harvard*).

Children:

89   i. Asa, born August 29, 1797. Family 29, page 41.
90   ii. Ethan, born February 27, 1799. Family 29a, page 41.
91   iii. Elizabeth, born March 13, 1804; married Thomas Taylor of Hancock, N. H., September 28, 1825.

FIFTH GENERATION

FIFTH GENERATION

FAMILY 17.

See page 29.

70. Nathan⁵ Daby (*Joseph, Joseph,³ John,² Thomas¹*), born August 4, 1766; married **Susan (Suky) Thompson** of Sterling, Mass., September 9, 1790. They were married by William Nichols, Justice of the Peace of Leominster. Nathan Daby died July 27, 1836. His widow died in 1848. They resided in Lancaster and Andover, Mass., and Rindge, Vt. Nathan was in the Revolution (*Westminster Men in Revolution*).

Children, born in Leominster:

92	i.	Oliver, born December 29, 1791. Family 30, page 45.
93	ii.	Nathan, born June 26, 1792. Family 31, page 45.
94	iii.	Deliverance, born in 1796. Family 32, page 46.
95	iv.	Ephraim, born November 16, 1798. Family 33, page 46.
96	v.	Sophia, born December 1, 1800. Family 34, page 47.
97	vi.	Milo, born in 1802. Family 35, page 47.
98	vii.	Josiah, born July 4, 1805. Family 36, page 48.
99	viii.	Emily, born in 1808. Family 37, page 48.
100	ix.	Betsey, died young.
101	x.	Mary.

FAMILY 18.

See page 29.

74. Joshua⁵ Derby (*Joseph,⁴ Joseph,³ John,² Thomas¹*), born March 9, 1777; married **Olive Haws,** January 30, 1799. She was a daughter of Benjamin and Sarah (*Leland*) **Haws,** and was born April 29, 1780, in Leominster, Mass. Joshua Derby died December 4, 1845, in Leominster, of bronchitis. His widow died November 17, 1851, of typhoid fever, in Wrentham, and was buried in Pondville, formerly a part of Wrentham, now in the town of Norfolk, Mass. They were married by Rev. Francis Gardner in Leominster.

Children:

102   i. Henry, born July 22, 1799. Family 38, page 49.
103   ii. Elbridge, born December 27, 1801; died August 28, 1828.
104   iii. Eli, born February 4, 1805; died next day.
105   iv. Mary R., born June 30, 1806; died June 8, 1892; unmarried.
106   v. Olive M., born November 29, 1808; died February 13, 1865; married H. K. W. Pond.
107   vi. Sarah, born August 30, 1811; died October 30, 1814.
108   vii. Amos Leland, born June 2, 1815; died March 9, 1888; married Lucinda Fuller.
109   viii. Edmond, born September 28, 1817; died July 9, 1820.

FAMILY 19.

See page 29.

75. John[5] Derby (*Joseph,*[4] *Joseph,*[3] *John,*[2] *Thomas*[1]), born 1781; married **Mary (Polly) Glover**, December 20, 1800. She died August 14, 1854, in Leominster, aged seventy-eight years. She was born in Randolph, Vt. John Derby died January 15, 1848, of paralysis.

Children:

110   i. John, born May 17, 1801; known as Capt. John Derby; died October 16, 1871.
111   ii. Polly, born January 1, 1802.
112   iii. Edward Glover, born February 5, 1805. Family 38*a*, page 50.
113   iv. Ira, born May 17, 1806. Family 39, page 50.
113*a*   v. Mary, born May 17, 1808; married to John Pitts of Townsend, Mass., November 25, 1826. She died in New York City, leaving one son, Friend Pitts.
114   vi. Joseph, born July 28, 1811.
115   vii. Abigail, born July 3, 1814.
116   viii. Elizabeth, born August 3, 1816; married Frank Huntley, and went west in 1857.

FAMILY 20.

See page 29.

76. Demaris[5] **Darby** (*Joseph,*[4] *Joseph,*[3] *John,*[2] *Thomas*[1]), born in Leominster, Mass.; married **Abraham Daby** of Athol, Mass.,

May 30, 1806. He was a son of Nathan **Derby** of Acton, and *Abigail Pierce* of Lexington, Mass., and was born August 30, 1780, in Westminster. He died in Athol.

FAMILY 21.

See page 30.

79. **Benjamin**⁵ **Derby** (*Joseph,*⁴ *Joseph,*³ *John,*² *Thomas*¹), born in 1775; married **Dolly Chase**, November 24, 1799, in Leo‑ minster. They were married by Rev. Francis Gardner. She was born in December, 1782, and died January 7, 1851. He died April 1, 1851. He was a shoemaker by trade.

Children, born in Leominster:

117   i. Loring, born May 10, 1800.
118   ii. William Hale, born May 31, 1802. Family 40, page 50.
119   iii. Emory, born July 31, 1804; went to Woburn, Mass.
120   iv. Volney, born September 19, 1806. Family 41, page 51.

FAMILY 22.

See page 30.

81. **Joseph Hartwell**⁵ **Derby** (*Benjamin,*⁴ *Joseph,*³ *John,*² *Thomas*¹), born February 22, 1780; married **Jane Colburn**, August 15, 1800. They were married by Rev. Francis Gardner, in Leominster. She was a daughter of Nathaniel and Jane (*Stratton*) **Colburn**, and was born September 17, 1781. Her father, Nathaniel **Colburn**, was a Revolutionary soldier. She died March 7, 1866. He died June 26, 1855. Both died in Leominster, and are buried there.

Children, born in Leominster:

121   i. Harriet, born March 11, 1801. Family 42, page 51.
122   ii. Polly, born January 1, 1803; died unmarried.
123   iii. Tabitha, born May 21, 1805. Family 43, page 52.
124   iv. Haskell, born May 8, 1807. Family 44, page 53.
125   v. William, born March 9, 1809. Family 45, page 53.
126   vi. Gilman (Gilbert), born June 5, 1811. Family 46, page 54.
127   vii. Dennis, born April 7, 1813. Family 47, page 54.
128   viii. Leander, born July 18, 1815. Family 48, page 55.
129   ix. Rufus, born February 27, 1818; went west.

130   x. Miranda Jane, born December 21, 1821. Family 49, page 55.

131   xi. Sophronia, born January 30, 1825; died March 3, 1825.

FAMILY 23.

See page 30.

82. Thomas[5] **Derby** (*Benjamin,*[4] *Joseph,*[3] *John,*[2] *Thomas*[1]), born April 19, 1782; married **Mary Stone Hill,** May 25, 1806. They were married by Rev. Nathaniel Thayer, in Lancaster, Mass. She was born March 5, 1781, and died August 9, 1854. He died April 25, 1852.

Children, born in Leominster:

132   i. Stillman, born August 1, 1807. Family 50, page 56.

133   ii. David Stone, born November 16, 1809. Family 51, page 56.

134   iii. Charles, born November 10, 1811; died March 31, 1835.

135   iv. Doretha Maria, born August 16, 1813. Family 52, page 57.

136   v. Mary Ann, born January 13, 1817; died October 26, 1860; married George Sage; no children.

137   vi. Cephas, born March 14, 1819. Family 53, page 57.

138   vii. Sewall, born March 14, 1819. Family 54, page 57.

139   viii. Thomas, born April 26, 1821. Family 55, page 58.

140   ix. Benjamin, born June 16, 1823. Family 56, page 58.

141   x. Jemima Eliza, born April 28, 1828; died May 5, 1893, in Leominster.

FAMILY 24.

See page 30.

83. Lucinda[5] **Derby** (*Benjamin,*[4] *Joseph,*[3] *John,*[2] *Thomas*[1]), born in 1789.

Child:

142   i. Henry P. Derby, born July 26, 1811. Family 57, page 59.

FAMILY 25.

See page 30.

84. Fannie[5] **Derby** (*Benjamin,*[4] *Joseph,*[3] *John,*[2] *Thomas*[1]), born June 28, 1793; married **Levi Divoll,** May 17, 1808. He died July 24, 1824. She died April 6, 1873.

Children:

144   i. Mary Ann, born September 5, 1809; died June 4, 1898.
145   ii. Levi, born March 19, 1811; died January 29, 1888.
146 iii. Francis, born December 24, 1812; died December 26, 1875.
147   iv. Benjamin C., born January 9, 1815.
148   v. Sophronia, born July 12, 1817; died August 13, 1824.
149   vi. Oliver, born May 7, 1819; died September 13, 1820.
150 vii. Oliver, born February 21, 1822. Family 58, page 59.

FAMILY 26.

See page 30.

85. **Rebecca**[5] **Derby** (*Benjamin,*[4] *Joseph,*[3] *John,*[2] *Thomas*[1]), born in May, 1797; married **Ebenezer Davis,** May 15, 1814. They were married by William Nichols, Justice of the Peace. Ebenezer Davis was born in New Salem, Mass., and buried in Lancaster, Mass. Rebecca Derby Davis afterward married Priest, and died in Lancaster, Mass., January 19, 1858, aged sixty-one years, eight months.

Children, by first husband (births of the first six are on the Leominster Records):

151   i. Nathan, born November 5, 1814; killed on the cars.
152   ii. John, born April 3, 1817; died, aged seventy-five years.
153 iii. Rufus, born October 11, 1819.
154   iv. Angeline, born October 26, 1821; recorded as Anny.
155   v. Arvilla, born in 1823; recorded as Orvilla; died in March, 1825.
156   vi. Albert Gallatin, born July 19, 1827.
157 vii. Cordelia.
158 viii. Hannah.
159   ix. James.
160   x. Theodore Lyman, born in 1841; died March 22, 1898, of consumption.

FAMILY 27.

See page 31.

87. **Simon**[5] **Darby** (*Simon,*[4] *Joseph,*[3] *John,*[2] *Thomas*[1]), born April 22, 1779, was married in Lancaster by Rev. Nathaniel

Thayer to **Lydia Johnson**, November 27, 1806. He died August 1, 1856. Lydia was born in 1788, and died March 2, 1858, of consumption. They lived in Leominster, Mass. Simon died of palsy. "Simon Darby made the first iron ploughs about the year 1800. Formerly our ploughs were made of more perishable material. Mr. Simon Darby constructed them of wood; and if men told the truth, his ploughs were very good; they would run without a holder, and turn the glebe flat over. But when the driver chose it, they would only cut and cover." (Wilder's *History of Leominster, Mass.*)

Children:

161   i. Esther, born in 1807; died in 1812.
162   ii. Josiah, born December 30, 1808. Family 59, page 60.
163   iii. Eliza, born April 22, 1812. Family 60, page 60.
164   iv. Sherman, born June 16, 1814; died October 11, 1836, in Lunenburg, Mass.
165   v. Nancy, born February 27, 1817. Family 61, page 60.
166   vi. Daniel Johnson, born July 3, 1820; died December 9, 1855, of consumption.
167   vii. Simon Johnson, born October 15, 1822; died September 29, 1825.
168   viii. Veranus, born July 11, 1825; died September 28, 1828.
169   ix. Anna Maria, born November 11, 1828; died June 1, 1836.

FAMILY 28.

See page 31.

88. **Sarah (Sally)**[5] **Derby** (*Simon,*[4] *Joseph,*[3] *John,*[2] *Thomas*[1]), born August 15, 1781; married **William Bennett Damon**, December 22, 1808. He was born March 16, 1754, in Reading, Mass., and died August 4, 1857. She died January 2, 1851.

Children:

170   i. Sally, born October 13, 1811; married Daniel Barnes.
171   ii. William, born January 12, 1814. Family 62, page 61.
172   iii. John, born December 17, 1815; married Cornelia Divoll.
173   iv. Josiah, born March 18, 1818; died in Stoneham, Mass.; unmarried.
174   v. Esther, born February 19, 1821; died September 13, 1857; unmarried.

FAMILY 29.

See page 31.

89. Asa⁵ Derby (*Asa,⁴ John,³ John,² Thomas¹*), born August 29, 1797; married, first, **Lucinda**; secondly, **Abigail Fisher**, June 6, 1838. She died May 5, 1846. He died February 14, 1887, in Lancaster, Mass. Asa Derby was Town Treasurer of Lancaster thirty-two years, from 1847 to 1879, when he declined further service, and was also treasurer of the Congregational Church Society, executor or administrator of many estates, and a director of the Lancaster Savings Bank. An incident illustrating the popular trust in the man, as well as his untiring willingness to serve his neighbors, was his appearance at the counter of the Lancaster Savings Bank when the Receivers of that bankrupt institution paid their first dividend in 1876, with eighty-five books of deposit, in most of which he had the interest of a trustee. He was a lineal descendant of John Daby, one of the original petitioners for the creation of the town in 1731. He served Harvard in the lower branch of the legislature in 1839, 1840, 1841. (Nourse: *History of Harvard,* page 157.)

Children, by first wife (Harvard Records):

175   i. Augustine W., born February 24, 1824.
176   ii. Sarah, born August 25, 1825; married Moses E. Fisher, September 17, 1846.

FAMILY 29A.

See page 31.

90. Ethan⁵ Daby, or Derby (*Asa,⁴ John,³ John,² Thomas¹*), born February 27, 1799; married, first, **Adeline Wetherbee**, January 21, 1829; secondly, **Lucy Hapgood Goldsmith**, April 30, 1834. She was born February 28, 1807, and died April 1, 1869. Ethan Derby died February 2, 1876.

SIXTH GENERATION

SIXTH GENERATION

FAMILY 30.

See page 35.

92. Oliver⁶ Derby (*Nathan,⁵ Joseph,⁴ Joseph,³ John,²
Thomas¹*), born December 29, 1791; married **Elizabeth Hadley.**
She was born May 28, 1794. He died in 1869, in Groton, Mass.
Children:

177   i. Calvin C., born November 10, 1812.
178   ii. Leander, born August 19, 1814.
179   iii. Irena D., born February 27, 1817.
180   iv. Edmon Deliverance, born July 23, 1819.
181   v. Susan A., born July 12, 1821.
182   vi. Mary Elizabeth, born June 24, 1823.
183   vii. Nancy B., born August 10, 1825.
184   viii. Sarah Jane, born January 6, 1827.
185   ix. Harriet Ann, born February 13, 1829.
186   x. George Oliver, born June 7, 1832.
187   xi. Frances Adeline, born July 31, 1836.

FAMILY 31.

See page 35.

93. Nathan⁶ Derby (*Nathan,⁵ Joseph,⁴ Joseph,³ John,²
Thomas¹*), born June 26, 1792; married, in 1811, **Betsey Thomas,**
daughter of Captain Philip and Mary (*Lafavor*) **Thomas.** She
died July 11, 1822. Captain Philip Thomas commanded the company from Rindge, Vt., at the Battle of Bunker Hill, and remained
in the siege of Boston until the close of the year 1776. Nathan
Derby married, secondly, **Betsey Balch,** daughter of Joel and
Betsey (*Stevens*) **Balch,** born April 27, 1800, in Andover, Vt.
She died November 10, 1871, in Andover.

Nathan Derby was a carpenter and was employed by Colonel
Gardner as master-builder in the construction of the Gardner
house and store. He lived in Chester, Vt. When he was eighty
years old, he came down from Vermont with a span of horses
alone and went to Boston, Mass., sold his horses, bought another

pair, and came back again all right, which was quite a smart thing for so old a man to do, there having been about one hundred and thirty-five miles of driving in all.

Children, by first wife:

188   i. Elmira, born January 24, 1816. Family 63, page 65.

189 ii. Eliza, born September 12, 1820; married Henry Sherwin. She died in 1849, having had one son, Roland.

190 iii. Francis T., born July 10, 1822. Family 64, page 65.

By second wife, born in Andover, Vt.:

191 iv. Lovina M., born July 24, 1826. Family 65, page 65.

192   v. Ira W., born November 12, 1829. Family 66, page 66.

193 vi. Charles W., born April 17, 1832. Family 67, page 66.

194 vii. Celinda Jane, born November 3, 1835. Family 68, page 67.

195 viii. Lorenzo Dow, born June 9, 1838; died in 1872.

196 ix. Leland Balch, born April 20, 1840. Family 69, page 67.

197   x. Eugene, born in February, 1843; died August 29, 1871.

FAMILY 32.

See page 35.

94. Deliverance[6] **Derby** (*Nathan,*[5] *Joseph,*[4] *Joseph,*[3] *John,*[2] *Thomas*[1]), born in 1796; married **Mary Wilson,** August 7, 1825.

Children:

198   i. May Janet, born in 1826.

199 ii. Eliza Ann, born in October, 1827.

200 iii. Hannah, born in 1829; died in 1832.

FAMILY 33.

See page 35.

95. Ephraim[6] **Derby** (*Nathan,*[5] *Joseph,*[4] *Joseph,*[3] *John,*[2] *Thomas*[1]), born November 16, 1798; married **Betsey Whitney,** November 24, 1825. She was born September 29, 1801, and died February 21, 1872. He died August 31, 1883, having resided in Westmoreland and Nashua, N. H.

Children:

201   i. Sarah E., born November 9, 1827; died July 1, 1844.

202 ii. Albert, born July 4, 1830. Family 70, page 68.

203 iii. Amos G., born August 4, 1831. Family 71, page 68.

204 iv. Harriet, born September 24, 1833.

205 v. George S., born February 7, 1839; married in Colorado; died about 1899.

206 vi. Anna E., born October 13, 1842.

FAMILY 34.

See page 35.

96. Sophia[6] Derby (*Nathan,*[5] *Joseph,*[4] *Joseph,*[3] *John,*[2] *Thomas*[1]), born December 1, 1800; married **Asa Prescott** of Westford, Mass., January 13, 1820. Asa was a son of Ebenezer and Hannah (*Wait*) **Prescott**, and was born October 15, 1800. He died November 29, 1885. Sophia died May 6, 1883.

Children, born in Westford:

207 i. Augustus Asa, born October 9, 1821; married Mary Ormsby of California.

208 ii. Julia Ann, born May 9, 1822. Family 72, page 68.

209 iii. Charles Abbot, born January 18, 1828; married Martha Larque. He died October 18, 1898.

210 iv. George Albert, born December 11, 1831; died May 2, 1869.

211 v. Melvin, born February 22, 1838; married Martha Nancook.

212 vi. Elias, born April 14, 1840.

213 vii. Martha Jane, born October 22, 1842; married Edward Chamberlain of New York.

FAMILY 35.

See page 35.

97. Milo[6] Derby (*Nathan,*[5] *Joseph,*[4] *Joseph,*[3] *John,*[2] *Thomas*[1]), born in 1802; married **Clara Cook,** November 27, 1833, in Fitchburg, Mass. She was a daughter of John and Anna (*Beals*) **Cook** of Winchenden, Mass. She was born January 26, 1810. He died June 8, 1851. They resided in Ashburnham, Mass. Their children were born there.

Children, born in Ashburnham:

214 i. Edward M., born May 16, 1836; died November 27, 1844.

215   ii. Wilbur M., born May 6, 1841. Family 73, page 69.
216   iii. Lizzie C., born March 29, 1848; married Willard Page;
        died September 21, 1867.

FAMILY 36.

See page 35.

98. Josiah[6] **Derby** (*Nathan,[5] Joseph,[4] Joseph,[3] John,[2]
Thomas[1]*), born July 4, 1805; married, February 2, 1832, **Betsey
Whitney,** daughter of Captain Lemuel and Betsey (*Hall*) **Whit-
ney,** born March 18, 1812, in Ashburnham, Mass. She died August
8, 1868. He died April 4, 1876. Both are buried in Ashburnham.
Children, born in Ashburnham:

217   i Sarah E., born May 23, 1833; died June 13, 1844.
218   ii. Mary E., born September 28, 1834; married William
        Flint, who died December 19, 1860, in the Army;
        married, secondly, Jonathan Edward Goodwin. She
        died September 7, 1887.
219   iii. Jane E., born July 30, 1836; married John H. Whit-
        ney, February 25, 1869.
220   iv. Emily A., born January 14, 1838; married George
        Fuller, July 29, 1860. She died in 1867.
221   v. Eurania, born April 30, 1839; married Boardman F.
        Warren, June 2, 1859. He died January 13, 1899.
        She died February 5, 1900.
222   vi. Josiah, born November 20, 1840; died June 17, 1844.
223   vii. Franklin C., born June 10, 1842; died July 20, 1842.
224   viii. Juliana R., born May 26, 1843. Family 74, page 69.
225   ix. Joseph H., born October 21, 1844; died May 26, 1866.
226   x. Harriet Elzina, born July 31, 1846. Family 75,
        page 70.
227   xi. Sarah Angeline, born September 6, 1848. Family 76,
        page 70.
228   xii. Francena E. (Fanny), born October 3, 1850; un-
        married.

FAMILY 37.

See page 35.

99. Emily[6] **Derby** (*Nathan,[5] Joseph,[4] Joseph,[3] John,[2]
Thomas[1]*), born in 1808; married **Dwell Whitney,** June 5, 1829,
in Andover, Vt. He was a son of Captain Lemuel and Betsey

(*Hall*) **Whitney,** and was born September 10, 1807, in Ashburnham, Mass. She died August 24, 1868. He died March 29, 1879.

Children (*births of the first two from the Townsend Records*):

229   i. Sarah Dwelle, born April 2, 1830; died August 15,
        1831.
230   ii. Mary Ann, born July 13, 1831; married John R. Hill.
231   iii. George Oliver, born November 10, 1833; married Caro-
        line E. Willard in 1858.
232   iv. Sarah Dwelle, born September 8, 1834.   Family 77,
        page 70.
233   v. Edwin, born January 6, 1836.   Family 78, page 70.
234   vi. Lewis, born July 9, 1838.   Family 79, page 71.
235   vii. Lemuel, born October 30, 1840.   Family 80, page 71.
236   viii. Emeline, born October 28, 1843.   Family 81, page 71.
237   ix. Augustus Gill, born September 26, 1845; married
        Martha S. Robbins.
238   x. Frances Etta, born September 30, 1849.

FAMILY 38.

See page 36.

102.   Henry[6] **Derby** (*Joshua,*[5] *Joseph,*[4] *Joseph,*[3] *John,*[2]
Thomas[1]), born July 22, 1799; married **Mary (May) White.**
She was born October 24, 1802. He died April 14, 1876. They
lived in Watertown, Mass.

Children:

239   i. Sarah Elizabeth, born October 29, 1824; died August
        27, 1865, of heart trouble.
240   ii. Elbridge Napoleon, born February 5, 1826; died
        November 10, 1846, of pneumonia.
241   iii. Lucy Ann, born February 10, 1828; died April 9,
        1832.
242   iv. William Henry, born February 7, 1830; died August
        5, 1856, of consumption.
243   v. Henry Clay, born August 27, 1833.
244   vi. Charles Edmund, born August 12, 1835; died January
        4, 1856, of epilepsy.
245   vii. Mary Melissa, born October 26, 1837; died September
        29, 1869, of heart trouble.

246 viii. Lucy Ann, born October 1, 1839; died February 4, 1890, of consumption.

247 ix. Frederick Elbridge, born September 25, 1841; died December 31, 1859, of consumption.

248 x. Herbert, born September 19, 1846; died May 27, 1892, of consumption.

249 xi. Elbert, born September 19, 1846; died February 20, 1847.

FAMILY 38A.

See page 36.

112. **Edward Glover**[6] **Derby** (*John,*[5] *Joseph,*[4] *Joseph,*[3] *John,*[2] *Thomas*[1]), born February 5, 1805; married **Laura Sherwin**, June 4, 1827. He died June 18, 1840 (*Townsend Records*).

Children, born in Townsend, Mass.:

249a i. Andrew Burr, born in 1831. Family 81a, page 72.

249b ii. Sara, married White, and lived in Petaluma, Cal.

249c iii. Edward M., married Nancy Kezar of Lunenburg, Mass., September 4, 1853, and removed to Petaluma, Cal., in 1877.

FAMILY 39.

See page 36.

113. **Ira**[6] **Derby** (*John,*[5] *Joseph,*[4] *Joseph,*[3] *John,*[2] *Thomas*[1]), born May 17, 1806; married **Louise Gerry**, January 17, 1828. They were married by Reverend Abel Conant, in Leominster, Mass.

Children:

250 i. Mary Jane, born April 4, 1829.

251 ii. Lucy Ann, born July 5, 1832.

252 iii. Louise Prescilla, born June 22, 1834; married Bancroft.

FAMILY 40.

See page 37.

118. **William Hale**[6] **Derby** (*Benjamin,*[5] *Benjamin,*[4] *Joseph,*[3] *John,*[2] *Thomas*[1]), born May 31, 1802; married **Sally Houghton**. They were married by Reverend Abel Conant, in Leominster. Sally was a daughter of Ephriam and Sally **Houghton**, and was born August 5, 1803, in Rindge, N. H. William Hale Derby died April 15, 1870. His widow died April 13, 1872.

Children:

253   i. George William, born July 19, 1833; married Louise
       Stone of Lancaster, Pa. He died in Marysville,
       Ky., about 1864.
254   ii. Sarah Elizabeth, born August 4, 1838. Family 82,
       page 72.
255 iii. Emeline Amelia, born November 15, 1840; resided in
       Sterling, Mass., in 1902.
256   iv. Theodore Augustus, born August 24, 1846. Family 83,
       page 72.

FAMILY 41.

See page 37.

120. Volney[6] **Derby** (*Benjamin,*[5] *Benjamin,*[4] *Joseph,*[3] *John,*[2]
Thomas[1]), born September 19, 1806; married **Mary Ann Divoll,**
July 12, 1826, in Leominster, Mass. She was born September
3, 1809, and died in 1898. He died September 14, 1858, in
Sterling, Mass.

Children, born in Leominster:

257   i. Reuben Augustus, born September 4, 1830. Family 84,
       page 73.
258   ii. John, born June 3, 1833.
259 iii. Emory Adams, born December 4, 1835. Family 85,
       page 73.
260   iv. Sophronia A., born July 14, 1837.

FAMILY 42.

See page 37.

121. Harriet[6] **Derby** (*Joseph Hartwell,*[5] *Benjamin,*[4] *Joseph,*[3]
John,[2] *Thomas*[1]), born March 11, 1801; married **William May,**
May 17, 1821, in Leominster, Mass. They were married by
Reverend Abel Conant. William was a son of James and Lydia
(*Smith*) **May.** He was born in 1796, in Leominster. He died
June 11, 1843. His widow died March 18, 1872. Both are buried
in Pine Grove Cemetery, Leominster. S. A. Drake (*History of
Middlesex County,* page 157), speaking of Maynard, Mass., says:
"Other industries of the town are the paper mills, first built by

William May, for the manufacture of paper by hand, about the
year 1820."

Children:

261   i. Sarah Ann, born November 13, 1822.   Family 86,
        page 73.

262   ii. William James, born February 13, 1825; died April
        13, 1825.

263   iii. Emeline Smith, born March 27, 1826; died March
        18, 1849.

264   iv. Dennis William, born September 17, 1832; died Feb-
        ruary 28, 1857.

265   v. Harriet Amelia, born July 15, 1836.   Family 87,
        page 74.

266   vi. Harriet Adelia, born July 15, 1836; died in February,
        1837.

FAMILY 43.

See page 37.

123. Tabitha⁶ Derby (*Joseph Hartwell⁵ Benjamin,⁴ Joseph,³
John,² Thomas¹*), born May 21, 1805; married **David Carter,**
October 11, 1832. They were married by Reverend Abel Conant,
in Leominster. David was a son of Silas and Rhoda (*May*) **Carter,**
and was born June 4, 1806, in Leominster. Tabitha died September 12, 1875. Her husband died October 15, 1889. He was a
farmer, owning a farm near the Lancaster line.

Children, born in Leominster:

267   i. Caroline Augusta, born August 19, 1833; died October
        4, 1862.

268   ii. Laura Jane, born March 2, 1836.

269   iii. Charles Franklin, born February 21, 1838.   Family 88,
        page 74.

270   iv. Rufus Harrison, born February 12, 1841; died Sep-
        tember 30, 1864, in Civil War.

271   v. Martha Maria, born September 5, 1842; died October
        6, 1843.

272   vi. Frances Ann, born October 2, 1845.   Family 89,
        page 75.

273   vii. Etta Sophia, born September 16, 1847.   Family 90,
        page 75.

274   viii. Marietta.

FAMILY 44.

See page 37.

124. Haskell[6] Derby (*Joseph Hartwell,*[5] *Benjamin,*[4] *Joseph,*[3] *John,*[2] *Thomas*[1]), born May 8, 1807; married **Eliza Colburn,** April 15, 1835, in Leominster. She was a daughter of Elnathan and Elizabeth (*Brooks*) **Colburn** of Leominster. She was born November 27, 1810, and died August 23, 1846. Haskell Derby married, secondly, **Roxanna Grant,** May 25, 1848, in Marshfield, Vt. They were married by Reverend Pinkney Frost. She was a daughter of Thomas and Lydia (*Crowinshield*) **Grant,** and was born January 16, 1815, in Cabot, Vt. Haskell died April 1, 1877; his widow, December 21, 1889; both in Leominster, where they are buried. He was a horn comb-maker.

Children, by first wife:

275   i. George Franklin, born August 30, 1839. Family 91, page 76.

276   ii. Ellen Eliza, born June 24, 1842. Family 92, page 76.

277   iii. Albert G., born August 22, 1846; died the same day.

By second wife:

278   iv. Artemus Crowinshield, born February 1, 1855; died September 14, 1856.

279   v. Mary Lizzie, born January 3, 1859; unmarried in 1904.

FAMILY 45.

See page 37.

125. William[6] Derby (*Joseph Hartwell,*[5] *Benjamin,*[4] *Joseph,*[3] *John,*[2] *Thomas*[1]), born March 9, 1809; married **Eunice Willard** of Sterling, Mass., November 1, 1832, in Lancaster, Mass. They were married by Reverend Nathaniel Thayer. William died April 15, 1870.

Children:

280   i. Julia Ann, born June 16, 1837. Family 93, page 77.

281   ii. Sophronia Caroline, born October 21, 1839; unmarried.

282   iii. Harriet Augusta, born in 1840. Family 94, page 77.

283   iv. Rosalina Maria, born in August, 1846; died February 19, 1849.

FAMILY 46.

See page 37.

126. **Gilman (Gilbert)**[6] **Derby** (*Joseph Hartwell,*[5] *Benjamin,*[4] *Joseph,*[3] *John,*[2] *Thomas*[1]), born June 5, 1811; married **Caroline S. Chase,** June 5, 1832. She was a daughter of Francis and Betsey (*Merriam*) **Chase** of Bolton, Mass. She was born March 6, 1814, and died February 5, 1875. Gilbert died May 26, 1880. Both are buried in Leominster. He was a maker of horn combs.

Children:

284   i. Sophronia Jane, born August 21, 1833. Family 95, page 78.

285   ii. Andrew Gilbert, born May 15, 1835. Family 96, page 78.

286   iii. Mary Caroline, born June 6, 1837. Family 97, page 79.

287   iv. Emma Elizabeth, born September 7, 1840. Family 98, page 79.

288   v. Wallace Wellington, born December 3, 1842; lost at sea about 1869 or 1870.

289   vi. Charlenia Cecelia, born October 14, 1848; died July 11, 1849.

290   vii. Ella Amelia, born July 25, 1853. Family 99, page 80.

FAMILY 47.

See page 37.

127. **Dennis**[6] **Derby** (*Joseph Hartwell,*[5] *Benjamin,*[4] *Joseph,*[3] *John,*[2] *Thomas*[1]), born April 7, 1813; married **Mary R. Woods,** May 14, 1840. They were married by Reverend Rufus P. Stebbins, in Leominster. Mary was a daughter of Joseph and Eunice (*Powers*) **Woods,** was born in 1815, and died September 27, 1852. Dennis Derby married, secondly, **Sally Woods,** October 27, 1853. They were married by Reverend Amos Smith. Sally was born in 1812, and was a sister of Mary R. Woods. Sally died November 15, 1875. Her husband died September 27, 1880. He was interested in the manufacture of horn combs, and was a very bright and intelligent man, though a great sufferer for many years with rheumatism.

Child:

291   i. Abbie Maria, born December 17, 1844; died September 8, 1852.

GILBERT DERBY.

From an Old Daguerreotype.

MR. AND MRS. LEANDER DERBY.

FAMILY 48.

See page 37.

128. Leander[6] Derby (*Joseph Hartwell,[5] Benjamin,[4] Joseph,[3] John,[2] Thomas[1]*), born July 18, 1816; married **Julia Reynolds,** October 24, 1842, in Mansfield, Conn. They were married by Reverend Henry Bromley. Julia was a daughter of Christopher and Charissa (*Huntington*) **Reynolds** of Mansfield. She was born October 8, 1821, in Mansfield. Leander Derby died October 24, 1851, in San Andreas, California. He went with a party from Leominster, Mass., to California, and in crossing the Isthmus of Panama, contracted a fever and only lived for a few days after reaching California. His wife's brother, George H. Reynolds, was one of the party. Mr. Derby was a horn comb-maker.

Children:

292   i. Viola Annette, born December 5, 1845. Family 100, page 80.

293   ii. Adelaide Charissa, born September 1, 1847. Family 101, page 81.

FAMILY 49.

See page 38.

130. Miranda Jane[6] Derby (*Joseph Hartwell,[5] Benjamin,[4] Joseph,[3] John,[2] Thomas[1]*), born December 21, 1821; married **Joel Sawtell,** May 16, 1850. They were married by Reverend C. M. Bowers, D.D. Joel Sawtell was a son of Joseph and Lucretia **Sawtell,** and was born May 15, 1809. His wife died August 30, 1882. He died July 16, 1888. Both are buried in Woodlawn Cemetery, Clinton, Mass.

Children, born in Clinton, Mass.:

294   i. Jane Lucretia, born April 23, 1851. Family 102, page 81.

295   ii. Mary Louise, born December 2, 1853. Family 103, page 82.

296   iii. Ann Eliza, born June 18, 1856. Family 104, page 82.

297   iv. Susan Stiles, born August 10, 1858. Family 105, page 82.

298   v. Joseph Henry, born April 11, 1861. Family 106, page 83.

299   vi. Walter Joel, born October 19, 1865.

FAMILY 50.

See page 38.

132. Stillman⁶ Derby (*Thomas,⁵ Benjamin,⁴ Joseph,³ John,²
Thomas¹*), born August 1, 1807; married **Elizabeth Richardson** of Billerica, Mass., January 8, 1837. They were married by
Reverend J. S. Sargent. Elizabeth died June 12, 1881. Stillman
died December 29, 1884. They lived in Medford, Mass.

Children:

300   i. Mary Elizabeth, born October 27, 1837, in Medford,
Mass.

301   ii. Ellen Maria, born November 11, 1839, in Buffalo,
N. Y.; died September 27, 1854.

302   iii. Cornelia Stanley, born February 10, 1843, in Buffalo,
N. Y.; died December 7, 1876.

303   iv. Charles Henry, born June 16, 1846, in Medford, Mass.;
died October 18, 1875. He was a clerk in the Charlestown Navy Yard for nine years, a position which he
held at the time of his death.

304   v. Stillman Gipson, born March 6, 1849, in Medford,
Mass.

FAMILY 51.

See page 38.

133. **David Stone⁶ Derby** (*Thomas,⁵ Benjamin,⁴ Joseph,³
John,² Thomas¹*), born November 16, 1809; married **Mary
Marianda Creede,** November 25, 1834. They were married by
Reverend John A. Albro, in Fitchburg, Mass. Mary was born
September 11, 1812, and died November 15, 1892, in Marlboro,
N. H. Her husband died November 21, 1899.

Children:

305   i. Dorothy Maria, born May 24, 1836; died May 27,
1856.

306   ii. Charles Henry, born October 9, 1838; died May 24,
1864; killed in the Civil War.

307   iii. Alice Lucretia, born April 28, 1841.

308   iv. Mary Frances, born July 22, 1851; died July 19, 1852.

309   v. Emma Jane, born June 28, 1854. ·

310   vi. Hannah Louise, born May 8, 1858.

311   vii. Francis Stone, born October 22, 1860.

FAMILY 52.

See page 38.

135. **Doretha Maria**⁶ **Derby** (*Thomas*,⁵ *Benjamin*,⁴ *Joseph*,³ *John*,² *Thomas*¹), born August 16, 1813; married **Jacob Craig.** He was a son of Amos and Abby **Craig**, and was born in February, 1818, in Ruminy, N. H. He died April 18, 1854. Doretha died March 31, 1897, in Leominster, Mass.

Children, born in Leominster:

312　i. Harrison, died January 29, 1863, in the Civil War. He served in the Seventh Massachusetts Battery, and fell in a skirmish near Blackwater, Va.

313　ii. Florence, died August 5, 1865.

FAMILY 53.

See page 38.

137. **Cephas**⁶ **Derby** (*Thomas*,⁵ *Benjamin*,⁴ *Joseph*,³ *John*,² *Thomas*¹), born March 14, 1819; married **Ann Eliza Nourse** of Bolton, Mass., April 7, 1842. They were married by Reverend Isaac Allen of Bolton. Ann was a daughter of Stephen and Sarah (*Houghton*) **Nourse.** Cephas died January 25, 1896, in Leominster. He was in the wood and lumber business, and served on the Board of Assessors six or seven years, and on the Board of Selectmen nine years.

Children, born in Leominster:

314　i. Mary Lewis, born January 14, 1843; died May 7, 1855.

315　ii. Charles Adfer, born December 9, 1844; died May 11, 1862, in the Civil War.

316　iii. George Herbert, born February 22, 1847. Family 107, page 83.

317　iv. William Graham, born October 22, 1854. Family 108, page 84.

318　v. Louis Henry, born July 25, 1857. Family 109, page 84.

FAMILY 54.

See page 38.

138. **Sewall**⁶ **Derby** (*Thomas*,⁵ *Benjamin*,⁴ *Joseph*,³ *John*,² *Thomas*¹), born March 14, 1819; married **Miranda Wood**, December 21, 1841. She was a daughter of George and Milly (*Hart-*

well) **Wood.** She died August 25, 1890. Sewall Derby died May 21, 1888.

Children, born in Leominster:

319   i. Adelia J., born January 25, 1845. Family 110, page 84.
320   ii. Ellen E., born January 7, 1847. Family 111, page 85.
321   iii. Albert E., born May 13, 1851. Family 112, page 85.

FAMILY 55.
See page 38.

139. Thomas⁶ **Derby** (*Thomas,⁵ Benjamin,⁴ Joseph,³ John,² Thomas¹*), born April 26, 1821; married **Laura Ann Whitney** of Leominster, April 1, 1841, in Brattleboro, Vt. They were married by Addison Brown.

Children:

322   i. Charles.
323   ii. Laura.
324   iii. George.

FAMILY 56.
See page 38.

140. Benjamin⁶ **Derby** (*Thomas,⁵ Benjamin,⁴ Joseph,³ John,² Thomas¹*), born June 16, 1823; married **Caroline Lincoln Stephenson,** August 1, 1852, in Townsend, Mass. They were married by Reverend Samuel Tupper. Caroline was a daughter of Galen Lincoln and Sarah (*Baldwin*) **Stephenson.** She was born April 3, 1835, in Boston, Mass., and died April 28, 1863, in Leominster. Benjamin Derby married, secondly, **Viola Heald,** October 25, 1868, in Temple, N. H. They were married by Reverend Isaiah Smith. Viola was a daughter of Eli and Susan (*Collins*) **Heald** of Temple, N. H. Benjamin Derby died August 29, 1903, in Leominster.

Children, by first wife:

325   i. Elizabeth Caroline, born April 21, 1853.
326   ii. Augusta Helen, born November 17, 1855. Family 113, page 85.
327   iii. Mary Louise, born July 13, 1858.

By second wife:

328   iv. Addie Eliza, born December 28, 1869. Family 114, page 86.
329   v. Russell Edward, born February 1, 1876.

FAMILY 57.

See page 38.

142. Henry P.[6] **Derby** (*Lucinda,*[5] *Benjamin,*[4] *Joseph,*[3] *John,*[2] *Thomas*[1]), born July 26, 1811; married, September 18, 1839, **Mary Ann Kilburn,** daughter of Daniel and Rachel (*McIntosh*) **Kilburn.** She was born in August, 1811, and died August 19, 1891. Henry P. Derby died March 4, 1870.

Children:

330   i. Henry K., born October 2, 1840; died January 5, 1862, in the Civil War.

331   ii. Mary Ann, born February 9, 1842. Family 115, page 86.

332   iii. Hiram, born October 4, 1843. Family 116, page 86.

333   iv. Sidney Harris, born October 26, 1845; died November 15, 1850.

334   v. Jane Lucinda, born December 1, 1847; died September 9, 1866.

335   vi. Lovina Rachel, born October 15, 1849; died May 16, 1867.

336   vii. Sarah Elizabeth, born February 23, 1852; married George Jefferson, December 25, 1891.

337 viii. Algernon Sidney, born January 2, 1855. Family 117, page 87.

FAMILY 58.

See page 39.

150. Oliver[6] **Divoll** (*Fannie Derby,*[5] *Benjamin,*[4] *Joseph,*[3] *John,*[2] *Thomas*[1]), born February 21, 1822; married **Susan P. Chute,** September 21, 1842, in Brattleboro, Vt. He died May 21, 1880. She was born November 26, 1825, and died January 12, 1894.

Children:

338   i. Oliver Franklin, born June 30, 1843. Family 118, page 87.

339   ii. Arthur Fitzerland, born December 21, 1844. Family 119, page 88.

340   iii. Joseph Homer, born April 4, 1846: died October 9, 1847.

341   iv. Susan Frances Josephine, born April 27, 1850. Family
        120, page 88.

FAMILY 59.
See page 40.

162. Josiah⁶ Darby (*Simon,⁵ Simon,⁴ Joseph,³ John,² Thomas¹*),
born December 30, 1808; married **Polly Hoar.** She was born
December 29, 1798, in Littleton, and died March 17, 1866, in Leominster. Josiah died January 1, 1852.

Children:

342   i. Julia Augusta, born May 21, 1833; died January 19,
        1873.
343   ii. Alden Waldo, born January 10, 1839. Family 121,
        page 88.

FAMILY 60.
See page 40.

163. Eliza⁶ Derby (*Simon,⁵ Simon,⁴ Joseph,³ John,² Thomas¹*),
born April 22, 1812; married **Joseph H. Whitney,** March 24,
1831. He was a son of John **Whitney,** and was born August 7,
1808, and died May 23, 1885. His wife died April 19, 1871.

Children:

344   i. Joseph A., born December 9, 1831.   Family 122,
        page 89.
345   ii. George H., born December 5, 1835; died December 20,
        1836.
346   iii. George H. S., born September 12, 1837.   Family 123,
        page 89.
347   iv. Sarah Maria, born April 22, 1840.
348   v. Charles J., born May 3, 1844; died January 10, 1872.

FAMILY 61.
See page 40.

165. Nancy⁶ Derby (*Simon,⁵ Simon,⁴ Joseph,³ John,²
Thomas¹*), born February 27, 1817; married **Warren Nourse** of
Lancaster, in June, 1840. He was born in 1809, in Bolton, Mass.
She died December 25, 1893.

Children, born in Leominster:

349   i. Ann Maria, born March 10, 1841; died April 8, 1844.
350   ii. Charlena, born April 26, 1843; died September 7, 1865.

351　iii. Charles, born December 10, 1846. Family 124, page 90.
352　iv. Lydia, born November 20, 1849. Family 125, page 90.
353　v. Edward, born April 14, 1855. Family 126, page 91.

FAMILY 62.

See page 40.

171. William[6] **Damon** (*Sarah Derby,*[5] *Simon,*[4] *Joseph,*[3] *John,*[2] *Thomas*[1]), born January 12, 1814; married, first, **Martha Litch;** secondly, **Lucy Bryant.**

Children, by first wife:

354　i. Frank.
355　ii. Jennette.
356　iii. Charles.
357　iv. George.

By second wife:

358　v. Lewis.
359　vi. Luther, married Jane Carter of England.
360　vii. Serena M., married Willard Perry.
361　viii. George B., married Mary Farwell.
362　ix. Sarah Adelia, married George W. Farwell.
363　x. Annie G., married Frank Gibson.
364　xi. Fred B., married Louise Carter.
365　xii. Walter M., married Alice Fernald.

SEVENTH GENERATION

SEVENTH GENERATION

FAMILY 63.

See page 46.

188. **Elmira**[7] **Derby** (*Nathan,*[6] *Nathan,*[5] *Joseph,*[4] *Joseph,*[3] *John,*[2] *Thomas*[1]), born January 24, 1816; married **Joseph Holt Peabody.** He was a son of Daniel and Betsey (*Holt*) **Peabody,** and was born November 24, 1815. He died April 2, 1889. Elmira died in 1838.

FAMILY 64.

See page 46.

190. **Francis T.**[7] **Derby** (*Nathan,*[6] *Nathan,*[5] *Joseph,*[4] *Joseph,*[3] *John,*[2] *Thomas*[1]), born July 10, 1822; married **Anna Thompson,** October 6, 1852, in New York City. They were married by Reverend Mr. Lounsbury. Anna was a daughter of John and Anna (*Thoms*) **Thompson,** and was born July 19, 1830. She died March 19, 1893, in Galesburg, Ill.

Children, born in Galesburg, Ill.:
366   i. Frank W., born August 5, 1854.
367   ii. William N., born May 26, 1859.
368 iii. Edward T., born December 31, 1861.
369   iv. Alice E., born April 22, 1867.
370   v. Mary L., born December 8, 1873.

FAMILY 65.

See page 46.

191. **Lavina M.**[7] **Derby** (*Nathan,*[6] *Nathan,*[5] *Joseph,*[4] *Joseph,*[3] *John,*[2] *Thomas*[1]), born July 24, 1826; married **Alonzo C. Clay,** August 15, 1854, in Galesburg, Ill. He was a son of John L. and Louisa M. (*Balch*) **Clay,** and was born February 13, 1828, in Chester, Vt. He died December 12, 1897.

Children, born in Galesburg, Ill.:

371   i. John L. Clay, born in June, 1855; died in September, 1862.

372   ii. Charles C., born September 6, 1856. Family 127, page 95.

373   iii. Martha M., born June 9, 1863. Family 128, page 95.

FAMILY 66.

See page 46.

192. Ira W.[7] **Derby** (*Nathan,*[6] *Nathan,*[5] *Joseph,*[4] *Joseph,*[3] *John,*[2] *Thomas*[1]), born November 12, 1829; married **Abigail Wilson,** August 20, 1857, at Kirkwood, Ill. They were married by Reverend Matthews of Monmouth, Ill. She was a daughter of Leonard **Wilson** of Whitehall, N. Y., and of Polly (*Winegar*) of Fort Ann, N. Y. Ira W. Derby was killed by a mowing machine July 25, 1892, in Wilton, Iowa. Mrs. Derby died February 10, 1904.

Children, born in Wilton:

374   i. Nathan W., born February 14, 1859. Family 128*a,* page 109.

375   ii. Ida J., born December 13, 1860; married D. S. Romig; died January 25, 1894.

376   iii. Eugene H., born October 5, 1866; resided in Wilton, Iowa, in 1903.

377   iv. Leonard S., born December 15, 1872. Family 128*b,* page 109.

FAMILY 67.

See page 46.

193. Charles W.[7] **Derby** (*Nathan,*[6] *Nathan,*[5] *Joseph,*[4] *Joseph,*[3] *John,*[2] *Thomas*[1]), born April 17, 1832; married **Frances M. Newell,** September 17, 1866, in Fruitland, Iowa. She was a daughter of Charles and Jeanette (*Wilson*) **Newell,** and was born March 1, 1850, in Mentor, Lake County, Ohio.

Children, born in Wilton, Iowa:

378   i. Ernest W., born December 16, 1868; married Tally Kerr. He died August 20, 1900.

IRA W. DERBY.

MRS. IRA W. DERBY.

HOME OF IRA W. DERBY, WILTON, IOWA.

379   ii. Stella M., born February 6, 1871; married Robert
       Fulton, and has three children, Ray, Mertle, and
       Charles.

380   iii. Jeanette, born March 20, 1882; resided in Wilton in
       1903.

FAMILY 68.

See page 46.

194. Celinda Jane[7] **Derby** (*Nathan,*[6] *Nathan,*[5] *Joseph,*[4]
Joseph,[3] *John,*[2] *Thomas*[1]), born November 3, 1833; married **William Frank Feltt**, September 1, 1859, in Andover, Vt. They were married by Reverend William S. Balch. William Feltt was a son of Abner and Hannah (*French*) **Feltt**, and was born September 28, 1828, in Chester, Vt. He died April 8, 1889, in Andover. Mrs. Feltt removed to Galesburg, Ill., in 1888, where she died October 7, 1902. She was buried in Andover, Vt.

   Child, born in Andover:
381   i. Ella L., born August 13, 1861.

FAMILY 69.

See page 46.

196. Leland Balch[7] **Derby** (*Nathan,*[6] *Nathan,*[5] *Joseph,*[4]
Joseph,[3] *John,*[2] *Thomas*[1]), born April 20, 1840; married **Eliza Viola Bensen,** December 25, 1863. They were married by Reverend William S. Balch, in Andover, Vt. Eliza was a daughter of McClure and Mary (*Warner*) **Bensen,** and was born August 24, 1845. She died April 19, 1884. Leland Balch Derby married, secondly, **Ida Abbie Jenkins,** August 21, 1889, in Weston, Vt. They were married by Reverend Moses Adams. Ida was a daughter of Charles Wesley and Laura (*Derby*) **Jenkins** of Peru, Vt., and was born August 5, 1866, in Landgrave, Vt.

   Children, by first wife:
382   i. Charles L., born February 23, 1869.   Family 129,
          page 95.
383   ii. Curtis H., born November 22, 1872.   Family 130,
          page 95.

Children, born in Andover, Vt.:

384   iii. Harry Wesley, born April 23, 1890.
385   iv. Newton Alonzo, born February 2, 1896.

FAMILY 70.

See page 46.

202.   Albert⁷ Derby (*Ephraim,⁶ Nathan,⁵ Joseph,⁴ Joseph,³ John,² Thomas¹*), born July 4, 1830; married **Martha P. Russell,** January 1, 1856. She was a daughter of David and Mary A. (*Wheeler*) **Russell,** and was born May 18, 1831, in Walpole, N. H.; died September 24, 1891, in Boston, Mass., and was buried in Bellows Falls, Vt. They were married by Reverend Albert Day. Albert Derby's occupation is that of a manufacturer of scythe snaths. He is a member of the firm of Derby & Hall.

Child, born in Bellows Falls, Vt.:

386   i. Minnie Frances, born April 13, 1861.

FAMILY 71.

See page 47.

203.   Amos G.⁷ Derby (*Ephraim,⁶ Nathan,⁵ Joseph,⁴ Joseph,³ John,² Thomas¹*), born August 4, 1831; married **Sarah F. Bennett,** September 3, 1857. They were married by Reverend Charles Greenwood. She was a daughter of Josiah and Sarah (*Goodrich*) **Bennett,** and was born January 20, 1834, in Westmoreland, N. H.; died January 21, 1903, in Encintas, San Diego County, California, and was buried in Bellows Falls, Vt.

Children, born in Westmoreland, N. H.:

387   i. Sarah Lizzie, born July 30, 1859.
388   ii. Martha Josephine, born March 23, 1868.
389   iii. Alice Bennett, born November 22, 1869.

FAMILY 72.

See page 47.

208.   Julia Ann⁷ Prescott (*Sophia⁶ Derby, Nathan,⁵ Joseph,⁴ Joseph,³ John,² Thomas¹*), born May 9, 1822; married **Oliver**

Fletcher Raymond. She died October 9, 1904, at 366 Main Street, Charleston, Mass.

Children, born in Charleston, Mass.:

390   i. Edward M.
391   ii. George Albert.
392   iii. Charles Oliver.
393   iv. Elma P.

FAMILY 73.

See page 48.

215. Wilbur M.[7] **Derby** (*Milo,*[6] *Nathan,*[5] *Joseph,*[4] *Joseph,*[3] *John,*[2] *Thomas*[1]), born May 6, 1841; married **Martha A. Page,** May 2, 1865, in Brattleboro, Vt. They were married by Reverend Addison Brown. Martha was a daughter of Warren and Mary (*Brown*) **Page,** and was born October 11, 1844. They resided several years in Rindge, and in Ashburnham, Mass., and afterwards in Florida, but returned to Ashburnham.

Children:

394   i. Warren M., born October 21, 1866, in Winchester, N. H. Family 131, page 96.
395   ii. Minnie M., born April 1, 1887, in Rindge, N. H. Family 132, page 96.

FAMILY 74.

See page 48.

224. Juliana R.[7] **Derby** (*Josiah,*[6] *Nathan,*[5] *Joseph,*[4] *Joseph,*[3] *John,*[2] *Thomas*[1]), born May 26, 1843; married **Joseph Nathan Day,** November 21, 1866, in Ashburnham, Mass. They were married by William Hatch of Fitchburg, Mass. Nathan was a son of Ithmar and Martha Azubah (*Wooley*) **Day,** and was born in Rockingham, Vt., January 3, 1841.

Child, born in Lancaster, Mass.:

396   i. Melvin J., born November 6, 1870. Family 133, page 96.

FAMILY 75.

See page 48.

226. Harriet Elzina[7] Derby (*Josiah,*[6] *Nathan,*[5] *Joseph,*[4] *Joseph,*[3] *John,*[2] *Thomas*[1]), born July 31, 1846; married, March 29, 1875, in Ashburnham, Mass., **Lafayette W. Pierce, Esq.,** of Winchendon, Mass., son of Ezekiel and Susanna (*Porter*) **Pierce,** who was born May 20, 1825, in Chesterfield, N. H. He died January 1, 1899, in Gainsville, Ga.

Child:
397   i. Thirza Belle, born July 11, 1876, in Winchendon.

FAMILY 76.

See page 48.

227. Sarah Angeline[7] Derby (*Josiah,*[6] *Nathan,*[5] *Joseph,*[4] *Joseph,*[3] *John,*[2] *Thomas*[1]), born September 6, 1848; married **Louis Morse** of St. Albans, Vt., October 10, 1874.

Child:
398   i. Fannie Eva, married Ernest Linwood Hill, M.D., in 1902.

FAMILY 77.

See page 49.

232. Sarah Dwelle[7] Whitney (*Emily*[6] *Derby, Nathan,*[5] *Joseph,*[4] *Joseph,*[3] *John,*[2] *Thomas*[1]), born September 8, 1834; married **Thomas Whitcomb,** April 20, 1859. He was a son of Silas and Louisa (*Lincoln*) **Whitcomb** of Marlboro, N. H. They resided in Ashby, Mass., in 1903.

No children.

FAMILY 78.

See page 49.

233. Edwin[7] Whitney (*Emily*[6] *Derby, Nathan,*[5] *Joseph,*[4] *Joseph,*[3] *John,*[2] *Thomas*[1]), born January 6, 1836; married **Eliza J. Cross,** in 1860. She died September 27, 1867, in Ashby, Mass. She was born in 1842. Edwin Whitney married, secondly, **Eliza-**

beth **Wheeler**, June 16, 1868. She was a daughter of Oliver **Wheeler** of Ashby, Mass.

Child, by first wife:

399   i. Fred.

FAMILY 79.

See page 49.

234. Lewis[7] **Whitney** (*Emily*[6] *Derby, Nathan,*[5] *Joseph,*[4] *Joseph,*[3] *John,*[2] *Thomas*[1]), born July 9, 1838; married **Mary Jane Lawrence.** She was a daughter of Leonard and Martha C. (*Hadley*) **Lawrence** of Ashburnham, Mass.

Children:

400   i. Frank.
401   ii. Charles.

FAMILY 80.

See page 49.

235. Lemuel[7] **Whitney** (*Emily*[6] *Derby, Nathan,*[5] *Joseph,*[4] *Joseph,*[3] *John,*[2] *Thomas*[1]), born October 30, 1840; married **Sarah Isabel Ward.** She was a daughter of William **Ward** of Ashburnham, Mass. Lemuel Whitney was in the Civil War. They reside in Pawtucket, R. I.

FAMILY 81.

See page 49.

236. Emeline[7] **Whitney** (*Emily*[6] *Derby, Nathan,*[5] *Joseph,*[4] *Joseph,*[3] *John,*[2] *Thomas*[1]), born October 28, 1843; married **Walter Lawrence,** November 17, 1868, in Fitchburg, Mass. They were married by Reverend Mr. Harding. Walter Lawrence was a son of Leonard and Martha C. (*Hadley*) **Lawrence,** and was born August 23, 1840, in Ashburnham, Mass. He died October 23, 1901.

Child:

402   i. Etta Belle, born January 9, 1879.

FAMILY 81A.

See page 50.

249a. **Andrew Burr**[7] **Derby** (*Edward Glover,*[6] *John,*[5] *Joseph,*[4] *Joseph,*[3] *John,*[2] *Thomas*[1]), born in 1831; married **Harriet M. Spaulding,** September 10, 1860. She was a daughter of Anson and Harriet (*Rugg*) **Spaulding,** and was born in Westminster, Mass., April 5, 1835. She died August 21, 1904, and her husband, December 6, 1896, both in Petaluma, Cal.

Children:

402*a* i. George W., born December 30, 1862; died August 20, 1870.

402*b* ii. Bertha E., born October 14, 1864; died July 26, 1867.

402*c* iii. Cora E., born September 27, 1867. Family 133*a,* page 97.

402*d* iv. Linda B., born January 17, 1871. Family 133*b,* page 97.

FAMILY 82.

See page 51.

254. **Sarah Elizabeth**[7] **Derby** (*William Hale,*[6] *Benjamin,*[5] *Benjamin,*[4] *Joseph,*[3] *John,*[2] *Thomas*[1]), born August 4, 1838; married **Josiah Carter,** December 27, 1860. Josiah died December 3, 1864. They had two children, who died young. His widow married, secondly, **Albert Carter,** in 1867. They live in Worcester.

Child:

403 i. Edith Persis, born January 31, 1869.

FAMILY 83.

See page 51.

256. **Theodore Augustus**[7] **Derby** (*William Hale,*[6] *Benjamin,*[5] *Benjamin,*[4] *Joseph,*[3] *John,*[2] *Thomas*[1]), born August 24, 1846; married **Mary A. Rogers,** May 30, 1871, in Nashua, N. H. They were married by Reverend J. O'Donnell. Mary A. Rogers was a daughter of Patrick and Ann **Rogers.** Theodore Augustus Derby has been married once or twice since, but we have no record. He lived in Providence, R. I., in 1902.

FAMILY 84.

See page 51.

257. Reuben Augustus[7] Derby (*Volney,*[6] *Benjamin,*[5] *Joseph,*[4] *Joseph,*[3] *John,*[2] *Thomas*[1]), born September 4, 1830; married **Sarah Offutt,** December 31, 1856, in Manchester, N. H. She was a daughter of George Offutt of Manchester. She died December 12, 1857. He married, secondly, **Sally W. Temple,** July 2, 1863, in Framingham, Mass. She died June 19, 1863. He married, thirdly, **Clara Light** of Hudson, Mass., in 1884. Reuben Augustus Derby was in the Civil War. He enlisted in Company C, Sixth Regiment of Massachusetts Volunteers in 1862 for nine months, and was discharged June 3, 1863. He re-enlisted August 23, 1864, in the Fourth Massachusetts Heavy Artillery, and was discharged June 10, 1865.

Children, by second wife:
404   i. George A.
405   ii. Irving E., died January 16, 1890.
By third wife:
406   iii. Lillian A., born June 17, 1886.
407   iv. Llewellyn L., born June 25, 1893.

FAMILY 85.

See page 51.

259. Emory Adams[7] Derby (*Volney,*[6] *Benjamin,*[5] *Benjamin,*[4] *Joseph,*[3] *John,*[2] *Thomas*[1]), born December 4, 1835; married **Laura Jane Carter,** October 8, 1873, in Stow, Mass. They were married by Reverend John S. Locke. Emory Derby and Laura Jane Carter were second cousins.

Child, born in Leominster, Mass.:
408   i. Walter Emory, born October 1, 1874; married April 26, 1905, in Leominster, Mass., Mary L. Hathaway.

FAMILY 86.

See page 52.

261. Sarah Ann[7] May (*Harriet*[6] *Derby, Joseph Hartwell,*[5] *Benjamin,*[4]*Joseph,*[3] *John,*[2] *Thomas*[1]), born November 13, 1822; married **Mark Kendall Brown**, in 1839. They were married by Reverend Rufus P. Stebbins in Leominster, Mass. He was a son of Odell and Lucy (*Belknap*) **Brown**, and was born November 17, 1819, in Sterling, Mass. He died May 1, 1877. She died March 24, 1894. Both are buried in Leominster.

Children, born in Leominster:

409   i. George William, born March 29, 1840. Family 134, page 97.

410   ii. Charles Summer, born October 31, 1841; died July 17, 1844.

411   iii. Sarah Frances, born April 13, 1844; died December 11, 1858.

412   iv. Lorenzo Edward, born March 18, 1846; died April 11, 1853.

413   v. Harriet Emeline, born May 22, 1848. Family 135, page 97.

414   vi. Martha Ann, born November 18, 1850. Family 136, page 98.

415   vii. Mary Ella, born April 7, 1853. Family 137, page 98.

FAMILY 87.

See page 52.

265. **Harriet Amelia**[7] **May** (*Harriet*[6] *Derby, Joseph Hartwell,*[5] *Benjamin,*[4] *Joseph,*[3] *John,*[2] *Thomas*[1]), born July 15, 1836; married **Charles Farwell Carter** of Leominster, April 25, 1860. They were married by Reverend Eli Fay. Charles Farwell Carter was a son of Nathaniel and Ann **Carter**, and was born June 8, 1827. He died April 4, 1882, in Leominster, Mass.

Children, born in Leominster:

416   i. Frederick Elmer, born January 25, 1862.

417   ii. Albert William, born October 28, 1865.

418   iii. George Dennis, born October 8, 1867.

FAMILY 88.

See page 52.

269. **Charles Franklin**[7] **Carter** (*Tabitha*[6] *Derby, Joseph Hartwell,*[5] *Benjamin,*[4] *Joseph,*[3] *John,*[2] *Thomas*[1]), born February 21,

1838; married **Laura Antoinette Sartelle,** May 6, 1868, in Leominster. They were married by Reverend William J. Batt. She was a daughter of Henry Everett and Laura Jane (*Miller*) **Sartelle.** She was born July 25, 1849, in Pepperill, Mass. Charles Franklin Carter was in the Civil War, in the Twentieth Army Corps under General Hooker. He was also with Sherman in his famous march to the sea.

Children, born in Leominster:

419   i. Irving Ralph, born November 11, 1869.

420   ii. Jessie Lillian, born August 26, 1875; married **William E. Lothrop.**

421   iii. Blanche Edith, born July 13, 1877; died December 24, 1902, of typhoid fever.

Jessie and Blanche were graduates of the Leominster High School, and Jessie of the Emerson School of Oratory, Boston.

FAMILY 89.

See page 52.

272. Frances Ann[7] **Carter** (*Tabitha*[6] *Derby, Joseph Hartwell,*[5] *Benjamin,*[4] *Joseph,*[3] *John,*[2] *Thomas*[1]), born October 2, 1845; married **James S. Willard,** August 31, 1868, in Fitchburg, Mass. James was a son of James and Charlotte B. (*Wileler*) **Willard.** Frances died October 15, 1887, in Leominster.

Children:

422   i. Frank, born in December, 1868, in Leominster.

423   ii. Charles, born in February, 1870, in Worcester, Mass.; died young.

424   iii. Mildred, born in 1883, in Worcester, Mass.; died in March, 1888.

FAMILY 90.

See page 52.

273. Etta Sophia[7] **Carter** (*Tabitha*[6] *Derby, Joseph Hartwell,*[5] *Benjamin,*[4] *Joseph,*[3] *John,*[2] *Thomas*[1]), born September 16, 1847; married **Ellery Wheeler.** She divorced him and married, secondly, **Theron J. Metcalf,** April 21, 1891, in Worcester, Mass. They were married by Reverend D. H. Stoddard. He was a son of

Jonathan and Juliette (*Graves*) **Metcalf**, and was born May 13, 1836, in Southampton, Mass.
No children.

FAMILY 91.

See page 53.

275. **George Franklin**[7] **Derby** (*Haskell,*[6] *Joseph Hartwell,*[5] *Benjamin,*[4] *Joseph,*[3] *John,*[2] *Thomas*[1]), born August 30, 1839; married **Catherine Richardson Goodrich,** December 10, 1860, in Sterling, Mass. They were married by Reverend E. B. Fairchild. Catherine was a daughter of Levi and Betsey (*Elliot*) **Goodrich,** and was born August 16, 1836, in Lunenburg, Mass.

Children, born in Leominster:

425   i. Henry Franklin, born August 15, 1861.   Family 138, page 99.
426   ii. Rose Delight, born October 22, 1863.   Family 139, page 99.
427   iii. Cora Amanda, born August 29, 1866.   Family 140, page 99.
428   iv. Albert Elmer, born September 10, 1875.   Family 141, page 99.

FAMILY 92.

See page 53.

276. **Ellen Eliza**[7] **Derby** (*Haskell,*[6] *Joseph Hartwell,*[5] *Benjamin,*[4] *Joseph,*[3] *John,*[2] *Thomas*[1]), born June 24, 1842; married **Michael Lynch,** April 16, 1864, in Fitchburg, Mass. They were married by Reverend Kendall Brooks.   Michael was a son of Patrick and Mary **Lynch,** and was born September 15, 1839, in County Clare, Ireland. He came to Leominster in 1848, where he is in the Express business.

Children:

429   i. Nellie Elizabeth, born September 22, 1865.
430   ii. Jennie Roxanna, born October 14, 1867.
431   iii. Eva Orlena, born February 21, 1869.
432   iv. Edwin Lorenzo, born January 17, 1877.

FAMILY 93.

See page 53.

280. Julia Ann[7] **Derby** (*William,*[6] *Joseph Hartwell,*[5] *Benjamin,*[4] *Joseph,*[3] *John,*[2] *Thomas*[1]), born June 16, 1837; married **Albert Jerome Roper** of Sterling, Mass., March 7, 1857. They were married by Reverend G. M. Bartoll. Albert Jerome Roper was a son of Houghton and Mary Esther (*Willard*) **Roper,** and was born July 4, 1832. After his death his widow married, secondly, **John H. Smith** of Charlestown, Mass., in December, 1866. They were married by Reverend G. M. Bartoll. John H. Smith was a son of David and Hulda (*Kelly*) **Smith,** and was born March 17, 1819. He died in 1877. His widow married, thirdly, **Charles Stone,** April 3, 1881, in Fitchburg, Mass. They were married by Reverend I. E. Wheelock. Charles Stone was born in 1818, and died December 15, 1890.

Children, by first husband:

433   i. Mary Esther, born August 17, 1860, in Lancaster, Mass.; married E. C. Brigham.

434   ii. Emma Jean, born June 20, 1863, in Sterling, Mass.; married Eben T. Cousins.

By second husband:

435   iii. William A., born June 10, 1875, in Lancaster, Mass.

FAMILY 94.

See page 53.

282. Harriet Augusta[7] **Derby** (*William,*[6] *Joseph Hartwell,*[5] *Benjamin,*[4] *Joseph,*[3] *John,*[2] *Thomas*[1]), born in 1840; married **Henry Wood** of Bolton, Mass.

Children:

436   i. Maria H., married Edward A. Ross of Leominster.

437   ii. Emma R.

438   iii. George H.

439   iv. Carrie E., married John McDonald of Nova Scotia. She died in 1899.

FAMILY 95.

See page 54.

284. Sophronia Jane[7] **Derby** (*Gilman,*[6] *Joseph Hartwell,*[5] *Benjamin,*[4] *Joseph,*[3] *John,*[2] *Thomas*[1]), born August 21, 1833; married **George L. Hull,** November 25, 1855, in Leominster, Mass. They were married by Reverend Amos Smith. George L. Hull was a son of George and Sara (*Lawton*) **Hull,** and was born July 4, 1832, in South Scituate, R. I. They went to California in 1867, where he was in the mill business. He died March 12, 1899, in San Francisco, Cal.

Children, born in Leominster:

440   i. Andrew Clifton, born May 10, 1858.   Family 142, page 100.

441   ii. Mary Louise, born August 20, 1860.   Family 143, page 100.

FAMILY 96.

See page 54.

285. Andrew Gilbert[7] **Derby** (*Gilman,*[6] *Joseph Hartwell,*[5] *Benjamin,*[4] *Joseph,*[3] *John,*[2] *Thomas*[1]), born May 15, 1835; married **Julia Ann Divoll,** February 28, 1853, in Danielson, Conn. They were married by Reverend George L. Chaney. Julia was a daughter of William and Dollie (*Houghton*) **Divoll** of Lancaster, Mass. She was born May 20, 1835, in Lancaster. Andrew Gilbert Derby died September 26, 1891, in Leominster. He had been engaged in the horn trade.

Children, born in Leominster:

442   i. Ida Augusta, born March 9, 1855.   Family 144, page 100.

443   ii. Herman Augustus, born October 17, 1856.   Family 145, page 101.

444   iii. Cora Frances, born August 10, 1858.   Family 146, page 101.

445   iv. Carrie Cecelia, born May 3, 1862.   Family 147, page 101.

446   v. Minnie Bell, born July 8, 1867.   Family 148, page 102.

447   vi. Walter Adams, born April 18, 1868.   Family 149, page 102.

448 vii. Maud Blanche, born November 18, 1870. Family 150, page 102.

449 viii. Ethel Amelia, born September 26, 1876. Family 151, page 103.

450 ix. William Carlton, born August 1, 1878. Family 152, page 103.

FAMILY 97.

See page 54.

286. **Mary Caroline**[7] **Derby** (*Gilman,*[6] *Joseph Hartwell,*[5] *Benjamin,*[4] *Joseph,*[3] *John,*[2] *Thomas*[1]), born June 6, 1837; married **Charles Sherman Peck** of Leominster, December 9, 1855. They were married by Reverend Amos Smith. Charles Sherman Peck was a son of Lee Grand and Laura (*Dimond*) **Peck** of Newton, Conn., and was born March 11, 1833. They went to California in 1860, where he has been engaged in Chinese transportation, or draying.

Children, born in San Francisco:

451 i. Frederick Neville, born May 18, 1863; died January 30, 1866.

452 ii. Harrison Gilbert, born February 13, 1866; died August 12, 1867.

453 iii. Laura Gertrude, born July 4, 1869. Family 153, page 103.

454 iv. Charles Noonan, born September 22, 1871.

455 v. Edward Eugene, born December 4, 1873. Family 154, page 104.

456 vi. Edith Bell, born December 4, 1873; died December 22, 1889.

457 vii. Frank Sherman, born December 11, 1876; died July 29, 1893.

458 viii. Ralph Fargo, born November 13, 1879; died July 19, 1882.

FAMILY 98.

See page 54.

287. **Emma Elizabeth**[7] **Derby** (*Gilman,*[6] *Joseph Hartwell,*[5] *Benjamin,*[4] *Joseph,*[3] *John,*[2] *Thomas*[1]) born September 7, 1840;

married **Edward Bartlett,** April 24, 1879, in Fitchburg, Mass.
They were married by Reverend J. T. Hewes. Edward Bartlett was
a son of Lela **Bartlett** of Northboro, Mass., and of Abigail *Boutrel*
of Reading. He was born April 24, 1833, and died February 13,
1898. His occupation was that of comb-maker. His widow died
November 23, 1899. Both died and are buried in Leominster.

Child:

459   i. Grace Isabell, born November 5, 1880; graduated from
        Mount Holyoke College in 1904.

FAMILY 99.

See page 54.

290. **Ella Amelia**[7] Derby (*Gilman,*[6] *Joseph Hartwell,*[5] *Ben-*
jamin,[4] *Joseph,*[3] *John,*[2] *Thomas*[1]), born July 25, 1853; married
Josiah M. Teel, in Oakland, California. They were married by
Reverend Horatio M. Stebbins. Josiah M. Teel was a son of
Thomas Henry and Lydia (*Russell*) **Teel,** and was born November 5, 1839, in Arlington, Mass. Mr. Teel went to California in
1881. They were married February 8, 1882. He engaged in Chinese
draying.

No children.

FAMILY 100.

See page 55.

292. **Viola Annette**[7] Derby (*Leander,*[6] *Joseph Hartwell,*[5]
Benjamin,[4] *Joseph,*[3] *John,*[2] *Thomas*[1]), born December 5, 1845;
married **Reverend Henry Bromley,** September 1, 1880, in Jersey City, N. J. They were married by Reverend Robert Bruce
Hull, D. D., assisted by Reverend A. S. Gumbart. Reverend Henry
Bromley was a son of Deacon Dewey and Lucretia (*Caswell*) **Brom-**
ley, and was born December 5, 1812, in Norwich, Conn. He died
April 20, 1896, in Brooklyn, N. Y., and was interred in Greenwood Cemetery. Mr. Bromley was a graduate of Hamilton Theo-
logical Institution, now Colgate University, in the class of 1834.
Viola graduated at Oxford Female College, Oxford, Ohio, in the
class of 1863. She is a member of the Daughters of the American

Revolution, of the Society of the Colonial Daughters of the Seventeenth Century, and of the Founders of Norwich, Ct.
No children.

FAMILY 101.

See page 55.

293. Adelaide Charissa⁷ Derby (*Leander,⁶ Joseph Hartwell,⁵ Benjamin,⁴ Joseph,³ John,² Thomas¹*), born September 1, 1847, married **William Francis Niles**, June 23, 1874, in Port Washington, N. Y. They were married by Reverend Charles Backman. William Francis Niles was a son of Joseph and Miriam Dorcas (*Hill*) **Niles**, and was born June 5, 1850, in Dracut, Mass. He died April 28, 1891, in Babylon, N. Y. Addie graduated at Oxford Female College, Oxford, Ohio, in the class of 1865.

Children:

460   i. Joseph Huntington, born April 2, 1875, in Leominster, Mass.

461   ii. Arthur Winslow, born March 20, 1877, in Leominster, Mass.; died October 2, 1903.

462   iii. Frederick William, born May 11, 1879, in Jersey City, N. J.

463   iv. Glenn Harold, born August 6, 1881, in Jersey City, N. J.

464   v. Charles Albert, born April 15, 1883, in Jersey City, N. J.

465   vi. Ruth, born July 28, 1884, in Jersey City, N. J., and lived 27 hours.

466   vii. Viola Adelaide, born October 2, 1886, in Jersey City, N. J.; died December 19, 1886.

467   viii. Edwin Reynolds, born April 19, 1888, in Babylon, N. Y.

468   ix. Alice Charissa, born June 17, 1889, in Babylon, N. Y.

FAMILY 102.

See page 55.

294. Jane Lucretia⁷ Sawtelle (*Miranda Jane⁶ Derby, Joseph,⁵ Benjamin,⁴ Joseph,³ John,² Thomas¹*), born April 23, 1851; mar-

ried **Horace Henry Lowe,** January 25, 1871, in Clinton, Mass.
They were married by Reverend Ivory F. Waterhouse. Henry
was a son of Henry Story and Sarah **Lowe,** and was born February 5, 1848, in Temple, N. H.

Children, born in Clinton, Mass.:

469   i. Horace Edwin, born May 18, 1872.   Family 155,
          page 104.
470   ii. Minnie Gertrude, born December 9, 1875. Family 156,
          page 104.
471   iii. Harold Henry, born May 25, 1886.
472   iv. Annie Mildred, born November 6, 1890.

FAMILY 103.

See page 55.

295. Mary Louise[7] **Sawtelle** (*Miranda Jane*[6] *Derby, Joseph,*[5]
Benjamin,[4] *Joseph,*[3] *John,*[2] *Thomas*[1]), born December 2, 1853;
married **Frank Smith,** June 24, 1875, in Clinton. They were married by Reverend Ivory F. Waterhouse. She died June 14, 1876,
and was buried in Woodlawn Cemetery, Clinton, Mass.

Child:

473   i. Edith May, born March 28, 1876; died August 22,
          1876, in Cambridge, Mass.

FAMILY 104.

See page 55.

296. Ann Eliza[7] **Sawtelle** (*Miranda Jane*[6] *Derby, Joseph,*[5] *Benjamin,*[4] *Joseph,*[3] *John,*[2] *Thomas*[1]), born June 18, 1856; married
Fred W. Straw, December 15, 1880, in Clinton. They were married by Reverend Charles Noyes. Fred was a son of William and
Caroline **Straw,** and was born April 2, 1854, in Lancaster, Mass.
His wife died April 16, 1881, in East Boston, Mass., and was
buried in Woodlawn Cemetery, Clinton, Mass.

No children.

FAMILY 105.

See page 55.

297. Susan Stiles[7] **Sawtelle** (*Miranda Jane*[6] *Derby, Joseph,*[5]
Benjamin,[4] *Joseph,*[3] *John,*[2] *Thomas*[1]), born August 10, 1858; mar-

ried **Harry D. Emery,** September 21, 1887, in Clinton, Mass. They were married by Reverend James C. Duncan. Harry D. Emery was a son of Nehemiah and Mary **Emery,** and was born July 11, 1860, in West Newbury, Mass.

No children.

FAMILY 106.

See page 55.

298. Joseph Henry[7] **Sawtelle** (*Miranda Jane[6] Derby, Joseph,[5] Benjamin,[4] Joseph,[3] John,[2] Thomas[1]*), born April 1, 1861; married **Annie Gardner Dodge,** July 21, 1889, in Haverhill, Mass. They were married by Reverend W. D. Bates. Annie Gardner Dodge was a daughter of Reuben George Washington and Betsey (*Jackson*) **Dodge**, and was born January 17, 1852, in Blue Hill, Maine. They resided at Haverhill in 1902.

No children.

FAMILY 107.

See page 57.

316. George Herbert[7] Derby (*Cephas,[6] Thomas,[5] Benjamin,[4] Joseph,[3] John,[2] Thomas[1]*), born February 22, 1847; married **Mary Ann Langer,** May 25, 1869. They were married by Reverend Edward Abbott of Cambridge, Mass. Mr. Derby is the inventor of the Derby Roll-Top Desk. His wife was born in 1850, near London, England; the daughter of Francis **Langer** and Jane (*Armstrong*).

Children:

474 i. Maude Alice, born November 7, 1871. Family 157, page 105.
475 ii. Mabelle, born April 2, 1873. Family 158, page 105.
476 iii. Edward Herbert, born May 26, 1875. Family 159, page 105.
477 iv. Herberta Anne, born December 10, 1882.
478 v. Francis Cephas, born July 4, 1886.
479 vi. Elmer Langer, born August 24, 1888.
480 vii. Dorothy, born February 6, 1892.
481 viii. George Weston, born February 28, 1896.

FAMILY 108.

See page 57.

317. William Graham[7] **Derby** (*Cephas,*[6] *Thomas,*[5] *Benjamin,*[4] *Joseph,*[3] *John,*[2] *Thomas*[1]), born October 22, 1854; married **Jennie M. Cawthorne,** May 14, 1879. They were married by Reverend W. A. Houghton, in Berlin, Mass. Jennie was a daughter of David and Catherine **Cawthorne** of Northboro, Mass. Mr. Derby was for a number of years a member of the Board of Assessors. William G. Derby married, secondly, **Harriet C. Tyler,** Marcy 31, 1897. They were married by Rev. James Bell, D.D., in North Leominster, Mass. Mrs. Derby was born September 7, 1857, in Lancaster, Mass., a daughter of Ansel **Tyler** and Harriet (*Parker*).

Children, by first wife:

482   i. Chester Cawthorne, born April 26, 1880. Family 160, page 106.

483   ii. Cephas Willie, born September 13, 1891.

FAMILY 109.

See page 57.

318. Louis Henry[7] **Derby** (*Cephas,*[6] *Thomas,*[5] *Benjamin,*[4] *Joseph,*[3] *John,*[2] *Thomas*[1]), born July 25, 1857; married **Isabel Cora Gallup,** October 5, 1881, in Providence, R. I. They were married by Reverend John C. Howlett. Isabel was a daughter of Orin and Mary **Gallup** of Lancaster, Mass. Louis Henry Derby died February 15, 1903, in Worcester, Mass.

FAMILY 110.

See page 58.

319. Adelia J.[7] **Derby** (*Sewall,*[6] *Thomas,*[5] *Benjamin,*[4] *Joseph,*[3] *John,*[2] *Thomas*[1]), born January 25, 1845; married **George W. Pierce** of Lunenburg, June 16, 1861. They were married by Thomas Billings, Justice of the Peace, Lunenburg. George W. Pierce was a son of Josiah and Nancy **Pierce.** Adelia J. (Derby) Pierce married, secondly, **Lyman W. Brown,** July 2, 1872.

Child, by first husband:

484   i. George E., born April 15, 1862.

By second husband:

485   ii. Edith H., born January 17, 1873. A twin.

486   iii. Everett, born January 17, 1873. A twin.

487   iv. Charles H., born September 1, 1874; married Nellie F. Johnson, June 16, 1897.

488   v. Mabel S., born July 23, 1876; married Louis H. Wheeler, February 15, 1893.

FAMILY 111.

See page 58.

320. Ellen E.[7] **Derby** (*Sewall,*[6] *Thomas,*[5] *Benjamin,*[4] *Joseph,*[3] *John,*[2] *Thomas*[1]), born January 7, 1847; married **Robert Holden** of Shirley, January 27, 1869. They were married by Reverend John B. Green of Chelsea. Robert was a son of Nathaniel and Catherine **Holden.**

FAMILY 112.

See page 58.

321. Albert E.[7] **Derby** (*Sewall,*[6] *Thomas,*[5] *Benjamin,*[4] *Joseph,*[3] *John,*[2] *Thomas*[1]), born May 13, 1851; married **Mattie Graves** of Boston, May 4, 1871, in Fitchburg, Mass. They were married by Reverend L. W. Spring. Mattie was a daughter of James and Martha A. **Graves.**

Child:

489   i. Albert L. F., born December 30, 1872; married Merlia Biby.

FAMILY 113.

See page 58.

326. Augusta Helen[7] **Derby** (*Benjamin,*[6] *Thomas,*[5] *Benjamin,*[4] *Joseph,*[3] *John,*[2] *Thomas*[1]), born November 17, 1855; married **George Herbert Lawrence,** December 16, 1880. They were married by Reverend William H. Savage, at Leominster. George was a son of Alfred and Carrie (*Streeter*) **Lawrence,** and was born September 13, 1857. He died February 25, 1898.

Children, born in Leominster:

490   i. Marion Augusta, born November 14, 1885.
491   ii. Raymond Clifton, born October 5, 1887.

FAMILY 114.

See page 58.

328. Addie Eliza[7] Derby *(Benjamin,[6] Thomas,[5] Benjamin,[4] Joseph,[3] John,[2] Thomas[1])*, born December 28, 1869; married **Ernest Maitland Benjamin Smith**, December 25, 1892, in Fitchburg, Mass. They were married by Reverend C. S. Brooks.

Children:

492   i. Nelson Ernest, born April 19, 1894.
493   ii. Helen Viola, born August 2, 1895.

FAMILY 115.

See page 59.

331. Mary Ann[7] Derby *(Henry P.,[6] Lucinda,[5] Benjamin,[4] Joseph,[3] John,[2] Thomas[1])*, born February 9, 1842; married **George W. Lovering**, October 23, 1869, in Shirley, Mass. They were married by Reverend A. J. Dutton. George was a son of Jonas and Rebecca *(Lovejoy)* **Lovering** of Andover, Mass.

Children:

494   i. George Sumner, born July 16, 1871.
495   ii. Arthur Frederick, born March 11, 1873. Family 161, page 106.
496   iii. Newton Oscar, born September 5, 1874. Family 162, page 106.
497   iv. Joseph Almon, born March 24, 1876.
498   v. Lavina Mary, born January 18, 1880.
499   vi. Mabel Lizzie, born May 14, 1882.
500   vii. A baby, born and died in December, 1884.

FAMILY 116.

See page 59.

332. Hiram[7] Derby *(Henry P.,[6] Lucinda,[5] Benjamin,[4] Joseph,[3] John,[2] Thomas[1])*, born October 4, 1843; married **Mary Elizabeth Donald**, October 4, 1866. They were married by Reverend J. B.

Green. Mary Elizabeth Donald was a daughter of Daniel and Catherine Donald of Boston, Mass. She was bdrn December 23, 1842; died July 2, 1903, at Fitzwilliam, N. H., and was buried in Evergreen Cemetery, Leominster, Mass.

Children:

501 i. Henry Kilburn, born August 8, 1867, in Leominster. Family 163, page 106.

502 ii. Ida Jane, born April 15, 1869, in Lunenburg, Mass.

503 iii. Lila Ann, born November 30, 1870, in Lunenburg, Mass.

504 iv. Edwin Hiram, born September 18, 1872, in Lunenburg, Mass. Family 164, page 107.

505 v. Mary Elizabeth, born August 13, 1874, in Lunenburg, Mass. Family 165, page 107.

506 vi. Nellie Centennial, born August 5, 1876, in Lunenburg, Mass. Family 166, page 107.

507 vii. Alvah James, born June 22, 1878, in Lunenburg, Mass.

508 viii. Augusta Caroline, born December 24, 1880, in Lunenburg, Mass.

509 ix. Elsie Emma, born January 4, 1884, in Fitzwilliam, N. H.

FAMILY 117.

See page 59.

337. Algernon Sidney[7] Derby (*Henry P.,[6] Lucinda,[5] Benjamin,[4] Joseph,[3] John,[2] Thomas[1]*), born January 2, 1855; married **Mrs. Louise McNamara** of Boston, Mass., December 31, 1878. They were married by Reverend W. H. Savage. Algernon Sidney Derby died December 16, 1880, in Fitzwilliam, N. H.

FAMILY 118.

See page 59.

338. Oliver Franklin[7] Divoll (*Oliver[6] Divoll, Fannie[5] Derby, Benjamin,[4] Joseph,[3] John,[2] Thomas[1]*), born June 30, 1843; married **Carrie A. Davis,** April 30, 1868.

Children:

510 i. Joseph Franklin, born January 27, 1870.

511 ii. Maud Josephine, born November 30, 1877.

88 DERBY GENEALOGY

512 iii. Harry Alden, born May 4, 1880.
513 iv. Willie Elmer, born July 25, 1882.

FAMILY 119.

See page 59.

339. Arthur Fitzerland⁷ Divoll (*Oliver⁶ Divoll, Fannie⁵ Derby, Benjamin,⁴ Joseph,³ John,² Thomas¹*), born December 21, 1844; married **Lizzie Baldwin,** May 1, 1870. He died December 22, 1888.

Children:
514 i. Herbert Arthur, born April 26, 1871.
515 ii. Cora A., born November 19, 1873.
516 iii. Charles H., born August 5, 1875.
517 iv. Susan J., born September 2, 1878; died January 10, 1896.

FAMILY 120.

See page 60.

341. Susan Frances Josephine⁷ Divoll (*Oliver⁶ Divoll, Fannie⁵ Derby, Benjamin,⁴ Joseph,³ John,² Thomas¹*), born April 27, 1850; married **Oren H. Smith,** December 25, 1868. She died October 26, 1875.

Children:
518 i. Artie Henry, born May 19, 1870; died September 2, 1870.
519 ii. Inez Josephine, born May 27, 1872.
520 iii. Willie A., born June 28, 1873.
521 iv. Bertha Susan, born August 26, 1875.

FAMILY 121.

See page 60.

343. Alden Waldo⁷ Derby (*Josiah,⁶ Simon,⁵ Simon,⁴ Joseph,³ John,² Thomas¹*), born January 10, 1839; married **Eliza Ann Robbins,** February 20, 1862. The ceremony was performed by Reverend Eli Fay. Eliza Ann Robbins was a daughter of Ephraim and Eliza **Robbins.** She died February 16, 1881. Alden Waldo Derby married, secondly, **Mrs. Annie R. (Melvin) Rand,** January 8, 1882, in Worcester, Mass. They were married by Reverend

M. P. Fairfield, D. D. She was a daughter of James and Harriet **Melvin** of Harvard, Mass.

Children, born in Leominster, by first wife:

522   i. Helen Louise, born April 25, 1866; died June 6, 1884.

523   ii. Emma Angelia, born May 27, 1868.   Family 167, page 108.

524   iii. Anna Maria, born August 31, 1869; drowned June 25, 1889.

525   iv. Alice Eliza, born November 6, 1870; died September 14, 1871.

526   v. Marion Julia, born June 27, 1873.   Family 168, page 108.

527   vi. Edith Frances, born February 11, 1875. Family 169, page 108.

528   vii. Florence May, born April 13, 1880.

By second wife:

529   viii. Ruth Mona, born May 6, 1883.

530   ix. Wilfred, born January 26, 1885.

531   x. Clifton, born January 5, 1887.

532   xi. Ralph Waldo, August 22, 1890.

533   xii. Everett Eugene, born October 6, 1892.

FAMILY 122.

See page 60.

344. Joseph A.[7] **Whitney** (*Eliza*[6] *Derby, Simon,*[5] *Simon,*[4] *Joseph,*[3] *John,*[2] *Thomas*[1]), born December 9, 1831; married **Elizabeth Blanchard**, March 27, 1856. He died December 21, 1899.

Children:

534   i. Henry Albert, born March 15, 1857; died February 8, 1859.

535   ii. Joseph Hiram, born February 1, 1861.

536   iii. George Amos, born August 2, 1865.

537   iv. Mary Eliza, born June 15, 1867; died July 28, 1867.

FAMILY 123.

See page 60.

346. George H. S. [7]**Whitney** (*Eliza*[6] *Derby, Simon,*[5] *Simon,*[4] *Joseph,*[3] *John,*[2] *Thomas*[1]), born September 12, 1837; married **Sarah Shattuck**, July 5, 1858. They separated, and he married,

secondly, **Hannah S. Eldridge,** September 1, 1870.   She died
August 1, 1887. He married, thirdly, **Sarah A. Abbott,** September
19, 1878.

   Children, by first wife:

538   i. George Henry, born May 23, 1859; died June 13, 1901.

539   ii. Alfreda Lucilla, born September 2, 1860; died April 1,
        1880.

540   iii. Eliza Ann, born April 14, 1863.

FAMILY 124.

See page 61.

351. Charles[7] **Nourse** (*Nancy*[6] *Derby, Simon,*[5] *Simon,*[4] *Joseph,*[3]
John,[2] *Thomas*[1]), born December 10, 1846; married **Martha
Pierce,** December 24, 1868. They were married by Reverend G. M.
Bartol of Lancaster, Mass.   Martha Pierce was a daughter of
James and Martha (*Warren*) **Pierce.**

   Children:

541   i. Charlena Hepsibeth, born January 29, 1870.   Family
        170, page 108.

542   ii. James Warren, born December 10, 1871; died Septem-
        ber 7, 1895.

FAMILY 125.

See page 61.

352. Lydia[7] **Nourse** (*Nancy*[6] *Derby, Simon,*[5] *Simon,*[4] *Joseph,*[3]
John,[2] *Thomas*[1]), born November 20, 1849; married **John Ordway,**
March 9, 1871. They were married by Reverend G. M. Bartol of
Lancaster, Mass. John Ordway was a son of Eben and Elizabeth
Ordway of Concord, N. H.

   Children:

543   i. Eva Gertrude, born February 5, 1872; married Clinton
        J. Conroy, May 21, 1891.

544   ii. Cora Mabel, born November 16, 1874; died in August,
        1876.

545   iii. Charles Edward, born September 19, 1877.

546   iv. Harry Alec, born April 23, 1880; married Maude La
        Fountain of Fitchburg.

547   v. Alfreda Ruth, born September 28, 1883.

548   vi. Bertha Myra, born December 23, 1886.

549 vii. Clesson Warren, born April 30, 1890.
550 viii. Walter Eben, born February 12, 1894.

FAMILY 126.

See page 61.

353. **Edward**[7] **Nourse** (*Nancy*[6] *Derby, Simon,*[5] *Simon,*[4] *Joseph,*[3] *John,*[2] *Thomas*[1]), born April 14, 1855; married **Clara Ordway,** May 12, 1875. She was a daughter of Eben and Elizabeth **Ordway** of Concord, N. H. Edward Nourse died October 8, 1889.

Children:

551   i. Herbert Clifton, born August 2, 1875.
552 ii. Ethel Edna, born July 29, 1877.
553 iii. Roswell Chester, born December 15, 1883.

EIGHTH GENERATION

EIGHTH GENERATION

FAMILY 127.

See page 66.

372. Charles C.[8] **Clay** (*Lavina M.*[7] *Derby, Nathan,*[6] *Nathan,*[5] *Joseph,*[4] *Joseph,*[3] *John,*[2] *Thomas*[1]), born September 6, 1856; married **Mary Hodge**, March 24, 1881. She was a daughter of William and Elizabeth **Hodge**, and was born in Galesburg, Ill.

Children, born in Galesburg, Ill.:

554   i. Myrtle, born February 21, 1883; married Cornelius Smith, in February, 1901, in Galesburg.

555   ii. Alonzo (Fritz), born October 5, 1884.

FAMILY 128.

See page 66.

373. Martha M.[8] **Clay** (*Lavina M.*[7] *Derby, Nathan,*[6] *Nathan,*[5] *Joseph,*[4] *Joseph,*[3] *John,*[2] *Thomas*[1]), born June 9, 1863; married **Samuel V. Stucky,** September 22, 1887, in Galesburg, Ill. He was a son of John A. and Margaret E. (*Norris*) **Stuckey.**

FAMILY 129.

See page 67.

382. Charles L.[8] **Derby** (*Leland Balch,*[7] *Nathan,*[6] *Nathan,*[5] *Joseph,*[4] *Joseph,*[3] *John,*[2] *Thomas*[1]), born February 23, 1869; married **Mrs. Laura (Cummings) Howard,** July 3, 1898, in Mechanicsville, Vt. They were married by Reverend George Clough. She was a daughter of William and Mina (*Preston*) **Cummings,** and was born in Wallingford, Vt., August 20, 1865.

Child, born in Andover, Vt.:

556   i. John Charles, born November 27, 1900.

FAMILY 130.

See page 67.

383. Curtis H.[8] **Derby** (*Leland Balch,*[7] *Nathan,*[6] *Nathan,*[5] *Joseph,*[4] *Joseph,*[3] *John,*[2] *Thomas*[1]), born November 22, 1872; married **Bertha Royce.**

Children:
557   i. A daughter.
558   ii. A daughter.

FAMILY 131.

See page 69.

394. Warren M.[8] **Derby** (*Wilbur M.,*[7] *Milo,*[6] *Nathan,*[5] *Joseph,*[4] *Joseph,*[3] *John,*[2] *Thomas*[1]), born October 21, 1866; married **Florida C. Bruce,** April 16, 1888, in St. Augustine, Florida. They were married by Reverend Charles C. McLane. She was a daughter of Elisha and Raphella (*Usina*) **Bruce** of Leominster, and was born in Fitchburg, Mass., April 25, 1868. Raphella Usina's father was a Spaniard, who came from Spain to Cuba, and afterwards settled in St. Augustine. Elisha Bruce was stationed in St. Augustine during the Civil War. He is a carpenter by trade, and in 1903 was superintendent in a toy shop in Leominster, Mass.

Child, born in Ashburnham, Mass.:
559   i. Bruce, born October 24, 1897.

FAMILY 132.

See page 69.

395. Minnie M.[8] **Derby** (*Wilbur M.,*[7] *Milo,*[6] *Nathan,*[5] *Joseph,*[4] *Joseph,*[3] *John,*[2] *Thomas*[1]), born April 1, 1887; married **Edward G. Lawrence** of Ashburnham, Mass., May 10, 1898. They were married by Reverend R. G. Floody, in Ashburnham. Edward G. Lawrence was a son of George W. and Ellen (*Reed*) **Lawrence,** and was born March 17, 1873, in Ashburnham.

Child:
560   i. Mildred Edith, born May 15, 1900, in Ashburnham.

FAMILY 133.

See page 69.

396. Melvin J.[8] **Day** (*Julian R.*[7] *Derby, Josiah,*[6] *Nathan,*[5] *Joseph,*[4] *Joseph,*[3] *John,*[2] *Thomas*[1]), born November 6, 1870; married **Emma A. Smith,** February 6, 1889, in Fitchburg, Mass. They were married by Reverend Mr. Whitteker. She was a daughter of Charles and Adelia (*Perkins*) **Smith** of Westminster, Mass.

Children:
561   i. Bernice Ellen, born January 27, 1890.
562   ii. Walter Earl, born November 12, 1892.

563   iii. Marion Emma, born November 12, 1892.
564   iv. Ruth Esther, born January 16, 1893.
565   v. Gladys Elizabeth, born July 28, 1895.
566   vi. Lillian Etta, born December 4, 1896.

FAMILY 133A.

See page 72.

402c. Cora E.[8] **Derby** (*Andrew Burr,*[7] *Edward Glover,*[6] *John,*[5] *Joseph,*[4] *Joseph,*[3] *John,*[2] *Thomas*[1]), born September 27, 1867; married **Emmet Benson**, November 25, 1886.

Children:

566*a*   i. Marcia, born March 5, 1888.
566*b*   ii. Rowena, born October 30, 1890.
566*c*   iii. Elwin, born February 18, 1893.
566*d*   iv. Velma, born June 20, 1896.
566*e*   v. Ruth Heath, born February 27, 1904.

FAMILY 133B.

See page 72.

402d. Linda B.[8] **Derby** (*Andrew Burr,*[7] *Edward Glover,*[6] *John,*[5] *Joseph,*[4] *Joseph,*[3] *John,*[2] *Thomas*[1]), born January 17, 1871; married **Henry S. Gutermute**, May 12, 1892.

Children:

566*f*   i. Sherwin R., born December 1, 1894.
566*g*   ii. Eunice, born August 28, 1899.

FAMILY 134.

See page 74.

409. George William[8] **Brown** (*Sarah Ann May,*[7] *Harriet*[6] *Derby, Joseph Hartwell,*[5] *Benjamin,*[4] *Joseph,*[3] *John,*[2] *Thomas*[1]), born March 29, 1840; married **Clara E. Carter**, February 15, 1881, in Leominster, Mass. They were married by Reverend William H. Savage. Clara was a daughter of Sumner and Damarius **Carter**, and was born March 31, 1840.

No children.

FAMILY 135.

See page 74.

413. Harriet Emeline[8] **Brown** (*Sarah Ann May,*[7] *Harriet*[6] *Derby, Joseph Hartwell,*[5] *Benjamin,*[4] *Joseph,*[3] *John,*[2] *Thomas*[1]), born May 22, 1848; married **Charles William Durant** of Leominster, March 19, 1867. They were married by Reverend Amos Smith in Leominster. Charles William Durant was a son of William and Marina (*Prescott*) **Durant**, and was born September 13, 1840, in Sutton, Mass. He died June 16, 1889, in Leominster; interment in Evergreen Cemetery. Harriet Emeline, his wife, died February 7, 1905.

Child:

567   i. Erva Kendall, born February 18, 1873, in Leominster.

FAMILY 136.

See page 74.

414. Martha Ann[8] **Brown** (*Sarah Ann May,*[7] *Harriet*[6] *Derby, Joseph Hartwell,*[5] *Benjamin,*[4] *Joseph,*[3] *John,*[2] *Thomas*[1]), born November 18, 1850; married **John H. Durgin** of Boston, Mass., February 4, 1873. They were married by Reverend George L. Chaney, in Boston. John H. Durgin was a son of John Y. F. and Abbie M. (*Walker*) **Durgin**, and was born September 5, 1844, in Dover, N. H.

Children, born in Boston:

568   i. Ella Bernoise, born December 4, 1874.
569   ii. Frances Winifred, born July 5, 1876; died October 23, 1900, in Rome, Ga.
570   iii. Bertha Allen, born July 6, 1881; died in Highlands, N. C.
571   iv. Christine May, born September 25, 1878.

FAMILY 137.

See page 74.

415. Mary Ella[8] **Brown** (*Sarah Ann May,*[7] *Harriet*[6] *Derby, Joseph Hartwell,*[5] *Benjamin,*[4] *Joseph,*[3] *John,*[2] *Thomas*[1]), born April 7, 1853; married **John Geary Wilson**, March 31, 1877. They were married by Reverend H. A. Wales. John Geary Wilson was a son of Edward and Sarah J. **Wilson**, and was born July 14, 1853. His wife died March 28, 1889, in Leominster.

Children, born in Leominster:

572   i. Christine Sarah, born December 7, 1880.
573   ii. Albert Dunham, born August 19, 1882; died December 15, 1888.

FAMILY 138.

See page 76.

425. Henry Franklin⁸ **Derby** (*George Franklin,*⁷ *Haskell,*⁶ *Joseph Hartwell,*⁵ *Benjamin,*⁴ *Joseph,*³ *John,*² *Thomas,*¹), born August 15, 1861; married **Helen Sargent** of Shirley, Mass., December 4, 1888, in Lunenburg, Mass. They were married by Fernando Brooks, Justice of the Peace of Lunenburg.

Children:

574   i. Alice Gertrude, born June 5, 1889.
575   ii. Maud Ethel, born July 28, 1890.

FAMILY 139.

See page 76.

426. Rose Delight⁸ **Derby** (*George Franklin,*⁷ *Haskell,*⁶ *Joseph Hartwell,*⁵ *Benjamin,*⁴ *Joseph,*³ *John,*² *Thomas,*¹), born October 22, 1863; married **Charles E. Gilson** of Lowell, Mass., December 11, 1889. They were married by Reverend E. B. Payne, in Leominster, Mass. Charles E. Gilson was a son of Abijah and Angeline (*McDonald*) **Gilson.**

Children:

576   i. Florence Agnes, born April 1, 1891.
577   ii. Cora Ethel, born August 6, 1894; died July 4, 1898.

FAMILY 140.

See page 76.

427. Cora Amanda⁸ **Derby** (*George Franklin,*⁷ *Haskell,*⁶ *Joseph Hartwell,*⁵ *Benjamin,*⁴ *Joseph,*³ *John,*² *Thomas,*¹), born August 29, 1866; married **Charles Payson Tyler,** June 23, 1887, in Pepperill, Mass. Charles Payson Tyler was a son of Joseph Augustus and Dollie A. (*Noyse*) **Tyler,** and was born September 5, 1865. They were married by Reverend James Mudge, in Pepperill.

Children:

578.   i. Ralph Augustus, born March 5, 1899.
579   ii. Hazel Dollie, born January 19, 1899.

FAMILY 141.

See page 76.

428. Albert Elmer⁸ **Derby** (*George Franklin,*⁷ *Haskell,*⁶ *Joseph Hartwell,*⁵ *Benjamin,*⁴ *Joseph,*³ *John,*² *Thomas*¹), born

September 10, 1875; married **Emma Maria Lillie** of Partridge-ville, Mass., May 27, 1896. She was a daughter of Sidney and Lucinda (*Haskins*) **Lillie**, and was born August 27, 1872.

FAMILY 142.

See page 78.

440. Andrew Clifton[8] Hull (*Sophronia Jane*[7] *Derby, Gilman,*[6] *Joseph Hartwell,*[5] *Benjamin,*[4] *Joseph,*[3] *John,*[2] *Thomas*[1]), born May 10, 1858; married **Mary Jane Fraser,** June 7, 1881, in Petaluma, Cal. They were married by Reverend Doctor Jones. Mary Jane Fraser was a daughter of John Bathold and Wilhelmina Henriette (*Nehls*) **Fraser.**

Children:

580   i. Gilbert Clifton, born May 27, 1883.

581   ii. Fronie Jane, born February 20, 1887.

582   iii. Ray Lawton, born April 21, 1890.

FAMILY 143.

See page 78.

441. Mary Louise[8] Hull (*Sophronia Jane*[7] *Derby, Gilman,*[6] *Joseph Hartwell,*[5] *Benjamin,*[4] *Joseph,*[3] *John,*[2] *Thomas,*[1]), born August 20, 1860; married **John Gill Pope** of Eufala, Ala., December 1, 1880. They were married by Reverend Horatio Stebbins, in San Francisco, Cal.

No children.

FAMILY 144.

See page 78.

442. Ida Augusta[8] Derby (*Andrew Gilbert,*[7] *Gilman,*[6] *Joseph Hartwell,*[5] *Benjamin,*[4] *Joseph,*[3] *John,*[2] *Thomas*[1]), born March 9, 1855; married **Augustus Granville Colburn,** July 9, 1872. They were married by Reverend W. A. Worthington. Augustus was a son of Joseph and Sally **Colburn,** and was born December 7, 1844, in Leominster. He died June 7, 1894, killed by accidentally stepping off a train in the dark.

Child:

583   i. Grace Cecilia, born January 11, 1874; married Bernis Edmund Lear, November 21, 1900. They were married by Reverend Frederick J. Gauld, in Leominster,

Mass. Bernis Edmund Lear was a son of Alverse
Darwin and Delia Ann (*Smith*) Lear, and was born
September 22, 1874.

FAMILY 145.

See page 78.

443. **Herman Augustus**[8] **Derby** (*Andrew Gilbert,*[7] *Gilman,*[6]
Joseph Hartwell,[5] *Benjamin,*[4] *Joseph,*[3] *John,*[2] *Thomas*[1]), born
October 17, 1856; married **Belle S. Whitcomb,** June 21, 1887.
They were married by Reverend H. A. Wales. Belle S. Whitcomb
was a daughter of Rix A. and Mary A. **Whitcomb** of Templeton,
Mass. They were divorced, and he married, secondly, **Jenette
Elizabeth Rutherford,** January 12, 1898. They were married by
Reverend G. R. Scott. Jenette Elizabeth Rutherford was a daughter
of John W. and Jenette (*Cranston*) **Rutherford,** and was born
March 11, 1868, in Madrid, N. Y. Mr. Derby died Sunday, March
3, 1903, in Leominster, of pneumonia. He was a member of the
Leominster Sportsmen's Association, and an ardent devotee of the
rod and gun. He was a comb-maker.

FAMILY 146.

See page 78.

444. **Cora Frances**[8] **Derby** (*Andrew Gilbert,*[7] *Gilman,*[6]
Joseph Hartwell,[5] *Benjamin,*[4] *Joseph,*[3] *John,*[2] *Thomas*[1]), born
August 10, 1858; married **Joseph Jackson King,** April 25, 1875.
They were married by Reverend William H. Savage, in Leominster.
Joseph was a son of Benjamin Franklin and Elizabeth Adams
(*Richardson*) **King,** and was born October 3, 1857, in Townsend,
Mass. He died December 16, 1891, in Leominster.

Children, born in Leominster:

584   i. Ethel Amina, born July 7, 1880.
585   ii. Florence Beatrice, born December 2, 1884.
586   iii. Clarence Jackson, born November 5, 1886.
587   iv. Walter Gilbert, born January 6, 1891.

FAMILY 147.

See page 78.

445. **Carrie Cecelia**[8] **Derby** (*Andrew Gilbert,*[7] *Gilman,*[6]
Joseph Hartwell,[5] *Benjamin,*[4] *Joseph,*[3] *John,*[2] *Thomas*[1]), born

May 3, 1862; married **Charles E. Smith** of Gardner, Mass., November 9, 1882. They were married by Reverend William H. Savage. Charles E. Smith was a son of Allen and Mary (*Hastings*) **Smith** of Gardner. He was born September 6, 1854, in Fitchburg, Mass. They resided in Keene, N. H., in 1902.

FAMILY 148.
See page 78.

446. **Minnie Bell**[8] **Derby** (*Andrew Gilbert,*[7] *Gilman,*[6] *Joseph Hartwell,*[5] *Benjamin,*[4] *Joseph,*[3] *John,*[2] *Thomas*[1]), born July 8, 1867; married **Ossian Goodale,** October 27, 1887. They were married by Reverend Edward B. Payne, in Leominster. Ossian Goodale was a son of Rowland Whiting and Lucy E. (*Haskins*) **Goodale,** and was born at Pratts Junction, Mass.

Children, born in Leominster:
588   i. Ralph Waldo, born April 23, 1888.
589   ii. Everett Burton, born November 9, 1890.
590   iii. Beatrice Mercedes, born April 10, 1894.

FAMILY 149.
See page 78.

447. **Walter Adams**[8] **Derby** (*Andrew Gilbert,*[7] *Gilman,*[6] *Joseph Hartwell,*[5] *Benjamin,*[4] *Joseph,*[3] *John,*[2] *Thomas*[1]), born April 18, 1868; married **Jennie Neely,** October 12, 1891. They were married by Reverend C. F. Rice, in Leominster. Jennie was a daughter of William and Agnes (*Parkill*) **Neely** of Newark, N. J. Walter Adams Derby served in the Spanish American War as Corporal of Company B, Sixth Massachusetts, United States Volunteers, mustered in May 13, 1898, at Fitchburg, Mass.

Children:
591   i. William Roy, born August 16, 1892, in Newark, N. J.
592   ii. Agnes Blanche, born August 16, 1892, in Newark, N. J.

FAMILY 150.
See page 79.

448. **Maud Blanche**[8] **Derby** (*Andrew Gilbert,*[7] *Gilman,*[6] *Joseph Hartwell,*[5] *Benjamin,*[4] *Joseph,*[3] *John,*[2] *Thomas*[1]), born November 18, 1870; married **Arthur Clesson Merriman,** June 6, 1888. They were married by Reverend Edward B. Payne, in Leominster. Arthur was a son of Clesson and Helen Mandana (*Mon-*

tague) **Merriman,** and was born June 11, 1868, in Northfield, Mass. He is in the comb business.

Children, born in Leominster:

593 i. Helen Montague, born September 23, 1889.
594 ii. Russell Gilbert, born March 2, 1892.
595 iii. Reginald Stanford, born July 5, 1896.

FAMILY 151.
See page 79.

449. **Ethel Amelia**[8] **Derby** (*Andrew Gilbert,*[7] *Gilman,*[6] *Joseph Hartwell,*[5] *Benjamin,*[4] *Joseph,*[3] *John,*[2] *Thomas*[1]), born September 26, 1876; married **Edwin Holmes** of Fitchburg, in August, 1892. They were divorced, and Ethel A. Derby Holmes married, secondly, **James Franklin Dennett,** January 5, 1898, a son of Jeremy B. and Eliza (*Odiorme*) **Dennett,** born in Taunton, Mass., January 8, 1873.

Child:

596 i. Granville Derby, born March 12, 1893.

FAMILY 152.
See page 79.

450. **William Carlton**[8] **Derby** (*Andrew Gilbert,*[7] *Gilman,*[6] *Joseph Hartwell,*[5] *Benjamin,*[4] *Joseph,*[3] *John,*[2] *Thomas*[1]), born August 1, 1878; married **Mina Louise Lincoln,** October 8, 1900. They were married by Reverend G. M. Bartoll, in Lancaster, Mass. Mina Louise Lincoln was a daughter of George T. and Ellen (*Sanderson*) **Lincoln.**

FAMILY 153.
See page 79.

453. **Laura Gertrude**[8] **Peck** (*Mary Caroline*[7] *Derby, Gilman,*[6] *Joseph Hartwell,*[5] *Benjamin,*[4] *Joseph,*[3] *John,*[2] *Thomas*[1]), born July 4, 1869; married **Herbert Atherton Page,** April 21, 1897, in Alameda, Cal. They were married by Reverend George R. Dodson. Herbert Atherton Page is a son of Nathaniel **Page** of New Bedford, Mass., and Emilia Amanda *Simonton* of Portland, Me. He is engaged in draying.

Children:

597 i. Kathryne Caroline, born July 1, 1898.
598 ii. Helen Gertrude, born October 18, 1900.

FAMILY 154.

See page 79.

455. Edward Eugene[8] **Peck** (*Mary Caroline*[7] *Derby, Gilman,*[6] *Joseph Hartwell,*[5] *Benjamin,*[4] *Joseph,*[3] *John,*[2] *Thomas*[1]), born December 4, 1873; married **Frances Blondine Pretorious,** September 10, 1895. She was a daughter of Frederick and Mary (*McCarthy*) **Pretorious.**

Children:

599   i. Bernice, born November 1, 1896.
600   ii. Charles Sherman, born June 5, 1898.

FAMILY 155.

See page 82.

469. Horace Edwin[8] **Lowe** (*Jane Lucretia*[7] *Sawtelle, Miranda Jane*[6] *Derby, Joseph,*[5] *Benjamin,*[4] *Joseph,*[3] *John,*[2] *Thomas*[1]), born May 18, 1872; married **Christina Wahl,** April 21, 1894, in Clinton, Mass. They were married by Reverend James C. Duncan. Christina Wahl was a daughter of Henry and Agnes **Wahl,** and was born July 7, 1875, in Clinton, Mass. They resided in Hopedale, Mass., in 1902.

Children:

601   i. Christine Vivian, born February 20, 1897, in Clinton, Mass.
602   ii. Meredith, born December 3, 1899, in Milford, Mass.
603   iii. Isabel Gertrude, born October 31, 1901, in Hopedale, Mass.

FAMILY 156.

See page 82.

470. Minnie Gertrude[8] **Lowe** (*Jane Lucretia*[7] *Sawtelle, Miranda Jane*[6] *Derby, Joseph,*[5] *Benjamin,*[4] *Joseph,*[3] *John,*[2] *Thomas*[1]), born December 9, 1875; married **Daniel Baker Clark,** June 14, 1899, in Clinton, Mass. They were married by Reverend James C. Duncan. Daniel Baker Clark was a son of Newton Ephraim and Kate (*Jones*) **Clark,** and was born November 3, 1870, in Keokuk, Iowa. They reside in South Framingham, Mass.

FAMILY 157.

See page 83.

474. Maud Alice[8] Derby (*George Herbert,[7] Cephas,[6] Thomas,[5] Benjamin,[4] Joseph,[3] John,[2] Thomas[1]*), born November 7, 1871; married **Wendell Maro Weston,** October 2, 1894. They were married by Reverend Edward Abbott of Cambridge, at Somerville, Mass.

Children:

604   i. Derby, born February 28, 1896.
605   ii. Amelia, born May 10, 1897; died November 16, 1897.
606   iii. Maro, born May 28, 1900.
607   iv. Stillman White, born March 13, 1902, in Winchester, Mass.

FAMILY 158.

See page 83.

475. Mabelle[8] Derby (*George Herbert,[7] Cephas,[6] Thomas,[5] Benjamin,[4] Joseph,[3] John,[2] Thomas[1]*), born April 2, 1873; married **Charles Frederick Chaurin,** November 9, 1896. They were married by Reverend Edward Abbott.

Children:

608   i. Dorothea, born September 21, 1897; died **August 24, 1898.**
609   ii. Doris, born February 13, 1900.
610   iii. Joseph Germain, born November 5, 1901, in Somerville, Mass.

FAMILY 159.

See page 83.

476. Edward Herbert[8] Derby (*George Herbert,[7] Cephas,[6] Thomas,[5] Benjamin,[4] Joseph,[3] John,[2] Thomas[1]*), born May 26, 1875; married **Mary Frances Stainford,** May 14, 1896. Edward died September 29, 1899. They were married by Reverend Edward Abbott.

Child:

611   i. Edward Herbert, born October 9, 1899.

FAMILY 160.

See page 84.

482. Chester Cawthorne[8] **Derby** (*William Graham,*[7] *Cephas,*[6] *Thomas,*[5] *Benjamin,*[4] *Joseph,*[3] *John,*[2] *Thomas*[1]), born April 26, 1880; married **Amy Holliday**, October 28, 1902, in Worcester, Mass. She was a daughter of William S. **Holliday.** They resided in Everett, Mass., in 1903.

FAMILY 161.

See page 86.

495. Arthur Frederick[8] **Lovering** (*Mary Ann*[7] *Derby, Henry P.,*[6] *Lucinda,*[5] *Benjamin,*[4] *Joseph,*[3] *John,*[2] *Thomas*[1]), born March 11, 1873; married **Mabel Kelly** of Ayer, Mass., August 8, 1898.

Children:

612   i. Roland, born February 14, 1899.

613   ii. Everett Waldon, born March 22, 1901.

FAMILY 162.

See page 86.

496. Newton Oscar[8] **Lovering** (*Mary Ann*[7] *Derby, Henry P.,*[6] *Lucinda,*[5] *Benjamin,*[4] *Joseph,*[3] *John,*[2] *Thomas*[1]), born September 5, 1874; married **Jennie Campbell** of Townsend, Mass., May 1, 1894.

Children:

614   i. Evabell Campbell, born June 18, 1895.

615   ii. Helen Hartwell, born July 5, 1900.

FAMILY 163.

See page 87.

501. Henry Kilburn[8] **Derby** (*Hiram,*[7] *Henry P.,*[6] *Lucinda,*[5] *Benjamin,*[4] *Joseph,*[3] *John,*[2] *Thomas*[1]), born August 9, 1867; married **Martha Arnold** of Terre Haute, Ind., April 25, 1894. They were married by Reverend R. V. Hunter.

Children:

616   i. Ethel May, born March 24, 1895, in Terre Haute, Ind.; died November 6, 1897.

617   ii. Helen, born December 18, 1896, in Terre Haute, Ind.; died November 12, 1897.

618   iii. Arthur Floyd, born December 6, 1898, in Chicago, Ill.
619   iv. Martha Jane, born December 16, 1900, in Chicago, Ill.

FAMILY 164.

See page 87.

504.   Edwin Hiram[8] **Derby** (*Hiram,*[7] *Henry P.,*[6] *Lucinda,*[5] *Benjamin,*[4] *Joseph,*[3] *John,*[2] *Thomas*[1]), born September 18, 1872; married **Nellie Augusta Thompson,** September 20, 1898. They were married by Reverend Albert W. Howes, in Fitzwilliam, N. H. She was a daughter of Samuel Bowman and Charlotte L. (*Willard*) **Thompson** of Monson, Mass., and was born May 5, 1874.

Children, born in Fitzwilliam, N. H.:
620   i. Vernon Hiram, born July 5, 1899.
621   ii. Roy Kilburn, born December 29, 1901.

FAMILY 165.

See page 87.

505.   Mary Elizabeth[8] **Derby** (*Hiram,*[7] *Henry P.,*[6] *Lucinda,*[5] *Benjamin,*[4] *Joseph,*[3] *John,*[2] *Thomas*[1]), born August 13, 1874; married **Henry Joel Whittemore,** December 21, 1895. They were married by Reverend David Foster, D. D. Henry Joel Whittemore was a son of Joel and Martha S. (*Walters*) **Whittemore** of New York City, and was born December 25, 1870.

Children, born in Wichendon, Mass.:
622   i. Eunice, born September 26, 1896.
623   ii. Inez Elizabeth, born February 17, 1898.
624   iii. Dexter Derby, born October 8, 1899.
625   iv. Lillian Walters, born December 6, 1900.

FAMILY 166.

See page 87.

506.   Nellie Centennial[8] **Derby** (*Hiram,*[7] *Henry P.,*[6] *Lucinda,*[5] *Benjamin,*[4] *Joseph,*[3] *John,*[2] *Thomas*[1]), born August 5, 1876; married **Chipman Mansfield Mawhinnie,** July 2, 1901. They were married by Reverend Arthur Wadsworth, in Fitzwilliam, N. H. Chipman Mansfield Mawhinnie is a son of David and Jane (*Craft*) **Mawhinnie** of Marces Bay, N. B.

FAMILY 167.

See page 89.

523. Emma Angelia[8] **Derby** (*Alden Waldo,*[7] *Josiah,*[6] *Simon,*[5] *Simon,*[4] *Joseph,*[3] *John,*[2] *Thomas*[1]), born May 27, 1868; married **Edward Amory James,** May 27, 1885, in Greenfield, Mass.

Children:

626   i. Helen Caroline, born June 4, 1887.

627   ii. Eva, born in 1889; died an infant.

628   iii. Florence Leland, born in March, 1896.

629   iv. Herbert Amory, born May 26, 1899.

FAMILY 168.

See page 89.

526. Marion Julia[8] **Derby** (*Alden Waldo,*[7] *Josiah,*[6] *Simon,*[5] *Simon,*[4] *Joseph,*[3] *John,*[2] *Thomas*[1]), born June 27, 1873; married **Lawrence Gove,** January 6, 1897. They were married by Reverend W. Greenman of Fitchburg, Mass. Lawrence Gove was a son of Lucien and Mary **Gove** of East Templeton, Mass.

Children:

630   i. Lester Harland, born February 4, 1898.

631   ii. Winfield Derby, born June 26, 1900.

FAMILY 169.

See page 89.

527. Edith Frances[8] **Derby** (*Alden Waldo,*[7] *Josiah,*[6] *Simon,*[5] *Simon,*[4] *Joseph,*[3] *John,*[2] *Thomas*[1]), born February 11, 1875; married **Henry J. Andrews,** December 7, 1899. They were married by Reverend W. Greenman of Fitchburg. Henry J. Andrews was a son of George B. and Lucy **Andrews** of Fitchburg, Mass.

FAMILY 170.

See page 90.

541. Charlena Hepsibeth[8] **Nourse** (*Charles*[7] *Nourse, Nancy*[6] *Derby, Simon,*[5] *Simon,*[4] *Joseph,*[3] *John,*[2] *Thomas*[1]), born January 29, 1870; married **William E. Foley,** May 4, 1893. They

Scott C. Derby.   Emma S. Derby.   Ray H. Derby.   Nathan W. Derby.

Ira H. Derby.

Home of Nathan W. Derby, Avoca, Iowa.

were married by Charles Joslin, Justice of the Peace of Leominster. William E. Foley was born in 1860.

Children:

632   i. Ernest William, born October 11, 1893.
633   ii. Ruth Edna, born July 29, 1895.
634   iii. Grace Evelyn, born October 17, 1897.

FAMILY 128A.

See page 66.

374. Nathan Wilson⁸ Derby (*Ira W.,⁷ Nathan,⁶ Nathan,⁵ Joseph,⁴ Joseph,³ John,² Thomas¹*), born February 14, 1859; married **Emma Stoughton,** December 24, 1884, in Osco, Ill. They were married by Rev. J. C. Stoughton. Emma was born in Osco, Ill., December 31, 1861, a daughter of Hardin **Stoughton** and Martha Jane *Foot.* Mr. Derby is a farmer.

Children:

555a   i. Ray Hardin, born September 29, 1885, in Wilton, Iowa.
555b   ii. Ira Hudson, born August 8, 1889, in Avoca, Iowa.
555c   iii. Scott Cyrus, born July 20, 1891, in Avoca, Iowa.

FAMILY 128B.

See page 66.

377. Leonard Samuel⁸ Derby (*Ira W.,⁷ Nathan,⁶ Nathan,⁵ Joseph,⁴ Joseph,³ John,² Thomas¹*), born December 15, 1872; married **Nellie F. Strong,** July 27, 1895, in Tipton, Iowa. They were married by Rev. C. L. Gould. Nellie was born June 15, 1879, in Marengo, Iowa, a daughter of William **Strong** and Ella *Raynor.* Mr. Derby is a druggist.

Child:

555d   i. Mae Abigail, born June 28, 1898, in Dexter, Iowa.

DERBYS UNPLACED

DERBYS UNPLACED

FAMILY 171.

635. Jonathan Derby, born July 4, 1726, O. S., in Hebron, Conn.; married **Abigail Dewey,** who was born September 3, 1730, O. S., in Hebron, Conn. He died January 19, 1794, in Orford, N. H. She died October 12, 1815, in Orford.

Children:

636   i. Rhoda, born February 19, 1749, O. S., in Hebron; died January 3, 1808, at Royalton, Vt.

637   ii. Abigail, born March 14, 1751, O. S., in Hebron; died February 22, 1772, at Lyme, N. H.

638   iii. Jonathan, born October 8, 1753, O. S., in Hebron.

639   iv. Simeon, born January 21, 1756. Family 172, page 113.

640   v. Ezra, born March 6, 1758, O. S., in Hebron; died in May, 1836, at Orford, N. H.

641   vi. Lavina, born March 12, 1760, O. S., in Hebron; died at Bradford, Vt.

642   vii. Lydia, born June 6, 1762, O. S., in Hebron; died at Orford, N. H.

643   viii. Lucy, born December 4, 1765, O. S., in Hebron; died December 3, 1784.

644   ix. Elizabeth, born April 28, 1768, O. S., in Hebron; died in September, 1842.

645   x. Apollos, born April 28, 1768, O. S., in Hebron. Family 173, page 114.

646   xi. Lemuel, born July 19, 1770, O. S., in Hebron.

647   xii. Dudley, born March 23, 1774, O. S., in Orford, N. H.; died in 1812, in Kingston, N. H.

FAMILY 172.

See page 113.

639. **Simeon Derby** (*Jonathan*), born January 21, 1756; married **Christianna Wells,** November 20, 1785, in Orford, N. H. She was a daughter of Thomas W. and Ruth **Wells,** and was born

May 7, 1760, in Chester, N. H. Simeon moved to Orford previous
to his marriage, and died there in May, 1836. His wife died
July 26, 1833, in Orford.

Children, born in Orford:

648   i. Lydia, born August 8, 1786.
649   ii. Betsey, born May 31, 1788.
650 iii. Sophia, born June 11, 1790; died February 21, 1824,
          in Orford.
651   iv. John, born March 19, 1794; died July 18, 1796,
          in Orford.
652   v. John, born August 5, 1796. Family 174, page '114.
653   vi. Thomas Wells, born December 20, 1800; died February
          5, 1801, in Orford.
654 vii. Christiana Wells, born June 29, 1803.

FAMILY 173.

See page 113.

645. Apollos Derby (*Jonathan*), born April 28, 1768, O. S.,
in Hebron, Mass.; married **Miss Kemp** of Pepperill, Mass. He
died in 1848. He made hay rakes.

Children:

655   i. Cyrus, a cabinet-maker, died unmarried, in Bridge-
          port, Vt., killed by a stone falling on him while
          stoning up a well.
656   ii. Jesse, married and had three sons and three daughters.
          He died, aged eighty-five years.
657 iii. Dexter, was a carpenter and joiner. He died in Au-
          burn, N. Y.
658   iv. Lemuel.
659   v. Chester, born June 15, 1800. Family 175, page 115.
660   vi. Melvin, born August 9, 1809. Family 176, page 116.
661 vii. Louise.

FAMILY 174.

See page 114.

652. John Derby (*Simeon, Jonathan*), born August 5, 1796;
married **Fidelia S. Freeman,** September 21, 1824. She was a

daughter of Caleb and Ruth (*Stores*) **Freeman**, and was born April 28, 1805, in Orford, N. H. John died May 16, 1857, in Orford, N. H. She died June 16, 1881, in Bridgewater, Vt.

Children:

662 i. Martha L., born August 31, 1825. Family 177, page 116.

663 ii. Henry B., born August 6, 1829. Family 178, page 116.

664 iii. Harriet, died in infancy.

665 iv. George G., born October 18, 1833; went to California in September, 1851; no children.

666 v. Francis Everett, born August 14, 1836. Family 179, page 117.

667 vi. Charles F., born August 22, 1840; died September 14, 1898, in Sanford, Me., leaving one son.

668 vii. Mary F., born February 12, 1842; died November 6, 1891.

669 viii. Rufus Augustus, born November 14, 1846; died February 14, 1897, at Bridgewater.

FAMILY 175.

See page 114.

659. Chester Derby (*Apollos, Jonathan*), born June 15, 1800, in Lynn, Mass., married **Polly Bixby,** in 1820, in Bridgeport, Vt. She was born May 15, 1803, and died February 1, 1860. Chester Derby died August 14, 1880, of blood poisoning.

Children, born in Bridgeport, Vt.:

670 i. Artemus Nickerson, born October 22, 1822; died October 16, 1823.

671 ii. Sally Malinda, born March 15, 1823; died July 18, 1865; married Lyman Allen.

672 iii. Maryette Sophia, born April 21, 1824; died September 11, 1825.

673 iv. Reuben Chester, born April 28, 1827. Family 180, page 117.

674 v. Louise Esther, born May 23, 1831; died June 12, 1832.

FAMILY 176.

See page 114.

660. Melvin Derby (*Apollos, Jonathan*), born August 9, 1809; married **Mary Woodward**, January 29, 1832, in Fairlee, Vt. He died September 17, 1877. She died May 15, 1889. Both died in Westmoreland, N. H. Mrs. Derby was born February 21, 1807, the daughter of Benjamin and Mary M. (*Murdock*) **Woodward**.

Children:

675 i. Susan P., born November 12, 1832, in Fairlee, Vt. Family 181, page 118.

676 ii. Edward M., born November 14, 1833, in Fairlee, Vt. Family 182, page 118.

677 iii. Isaac W., born October 2, 1835, in Fairlee, Vt. Family 183, page 118.

678 iv. Abigail M., born August 19, 1837, in Fairlee, Vt. Family 184, page 119.

679 v. Charles L., born March 23, 1840, in Westmoreland. Family 185, page 119.

680 vi. Jane E., born March 30, 1843, in Westmoreland. Family 186, page 119.

681 vii. Henry S., born May 8, 1845, in Westmoreland. Family 187, page 119.

682 viii. Sarah F., born April 25, 1847, in Westmoreland. Family 188, page 119.

FAMILY 177.

See page 115.

662. Martha L. Derby (*John, Simeon, Jonathan*), born August 31, 1825; married **Willard Y. Chase,** January 10, 1850, and removed to Craftsbury, Vt., in 1854. They subsequently went to Wisconsin.

No children.

FAMILY 178.

See page 115.

663. Henry B. Derby (*John, Simeon, Jonathan*), born August 6, 1829, died while in service during the Civil War at City Point, Va., in February, 1865.

Children:

683 i. Lucius, an electrician of Lowell, Mass.
684 ii. Frank, an electrician of Lowell, Mass.

FAMILY 179.

See page 115.

666. Francis Everett Derby (*John, Simeon, Jonathan*), born August 14, 1836; married **Susie Amelia Mills,** July 27, 1861, in Manchester, N. H. She was a daughter of Hezekiah and Susan (*Brown*) **Mills,** and was born June 1, 1841, in New London, N. H. She died September 20, 1898.

Children:

685 i. Eugene C., born March 7, 1867.
686 ii. Myrtle J., born October 21, 1870.
687 iii. George M., born December 7, 1872; died September 19, 1874.
688 iv. Pearl C., born March 3, 1887.

FAMILY 180.

See page 115.

673. Reuben Chester Derby (*Chester, Apollos, Jonathan*), born April 28, 1827; married **Betsey Ellen Grant,** August 28, 1858. They were married by Reverend Robert Taylor of Crown Point, Essex County, N. Y. She was a daughter of George and Phebe (*Miller*) **Grant,** and was born May 30, 1840. They moved to Crown Point in 1858, and resided at Ticonderoga, N. Y., in 1903. Her father, George Grant, born in 1774, she says, was a cousin of General U. S. Grant. Phebe Miller, her mother, was born in 1800, in Ticonderoga, N. Y.

Children:

689 i. George Grant, born April 18, 1869, in Waterloo, Iowa.
690 ii. Samuel Bixby, born May 14, 1873, in Ticonderoga, N. Y.
691 iii. Truman Perry, born July 30, 1875, in Ticonderoga, N. Y.

FAMILY 181.

See page 116.

675. Susan P. Derby (*Melvin, Apollos, Jonathan*), born November 12, 1832; married **Abial Stickney,** in January, 1852. They reside in Olney, Young County, Texas.

FAMILY 182.

See page 116.

676. Edward M. Derby (*Melvin, Apollos, Jonathan*), born November 14, 1833; married **J. Blake,** October 28, 1860. He was a member of the Fifty-Seventh Massachusetts Volunteers, and was killed in a charge at the battle of Spottsylvania, Va., May 12, 1864.

FAMILY 183.

See page 116.

677. Isaac W. Derby (*Melvin, Apollos, Jonathan*), born October 2, 1835; married **Arabella Heustis,** October 28, 1857. They were married by Reverend Rollin H. Neal, D. D., in Boston, Mass. She was a daughter of Gilbert T. and Martha (*Hodges*) **Heustis,** and was born December 16, 1834, in Westmoreland, N. H. She died in Dorcester, Mass. Capt. Isaac W. Derby writes: "I was in the service of the United States in the War of the Rebellion, in the Second Regiment, New Hampshire Volunteers, and First Regiment, Veteran Reserves Corps, in which latter organization I held a second lieutenant's commission, signed by Abraham Lincoln, President of the United States, and E. M. Stanton, Secretary of War, which I have framed at home. My rank as captain came from a commission held in the Volunteer Militia of Massachusetts. I lost my left arm in service at the first battle of Bull Run, July 21, 1861."

Children:

692　i. Freddie Walter, born September 7, 1860, in Westmoreland, N. H.; died an infant.

693　ii. Frank Fish, born July 23, 1862, in Keene, N. H.

694　iii. Mary Belle, born December 17, 1870. Family 189, page 120.

FAMILY 184.

See page 116.

678. Abigail M. Derby (*Melvin, Apollos, Jonathan*), born August 19, 1837; married **Henry E. Houghton,** June 3, 1859. They resided at Walpole, N. H., in 1903.

FAMILY 185.

See page 116.

679. Charles L. Derby (*Melvin, Apollos, Jonathan*), born March 23, 1841; married **Mrs. Susan Spaulding,** July 27, 1868. Charles was a member of the Fourteenth New Hampshire Volunteers in the Civil War. He resided at Westmoreland, N. H., in 1903.

FAMILY 186.

See page 116.

680. Jane E. Derby (*Melvin, Apollos, Jonathan*), born March 30, 1843; married **Edward M. Green,** June 14, 1868. They reside in Westmoreland, N. H.

Children:

695   i. Edward C., born September 26, 1869, in Fitchburg, Mass.; married Myra W. Burt, in 1891.

696   ii. Walter L., born July 9, 1872, in Fitchburg, Mass.; married Kate M. Carey, in 1895.

697   iii. Levi K., born April 2, 1877, in Fitchburg, Mass.; unmarried in 1903.

FAMILY 187.

See page 116.

681. Henry S. Derby (*Melvin, Apollos, Jonathan*), born May 8, 1845; married **Mrs. Lizzie A. Bruce,** May 6, 1871. They reside in Leominster, Mass.

FAMILY 188.

See page 116.

682. Sarah F. Derby (*Melvin, Apollos, Jonathan*), born April 25, 1847; married **Hobart Hazelton,** January 31, 1869. She died August 2, 1869, in Chester, Vt.

FAMILY 189.

See page 118.

694. Mary Belle Derby (*Isaac W., Melvin, Apollos, Jonathan*), was born December 17, 1870, and married **Ephraim Morton Paine**, March 9, 1891, in Chicago, Ill. He was a son of Eugene and Fedora M. (*Thompson*) **Paine**. He died in New Mexico January 6, 1894, and was buried at Jay Bridge, Me. Mrs. Paine married, secondly, **Jean Justus Van Derveer**, June 30, 1903, at Dorchester, Mass. He was born August 7, 1870, in New York City, a son of Joshua and Julia Dorothea (*Lemaire*) **Van Derveer**.

Child, by second husband:

698   i. Dorothea Arabella, born April 21, 1904, at Concord, Mass.

OWNER'S LINEAGE

OWNER'S LINEAGE

FIRST GENERATION

NAME...

NUMBER............   PAGES........AND..

SECOND GENERATION

NAME...

NUMBER............   PAGES........AND..

THIRD GENERATION

NAME...

NUMBER............   PAGES........AND..

FOURTH GENERATION

NAME...

NUMBER............   PAGES........AND..

FIFTH GENERATION

NAME...

NUMBER............   PAGES........AND..

SIXTH GENERATION

NAME...

NUMBER............   PAGES........AND..

SEVENTH GENERATION

Name...

Number.............   Pages........and..

EIGHTH GENERATION

Name...

Number.............   Pages........and..

NINTH GENERATION

Name...

Number.............   Pages........and..

TENTH GENERATION

Name...

Number.............   Pages........and..

ELEVENTH GENERATION

Name...

Number.............   Pages........and..

TWELFTH GENERATION

Name...

Number.............   Pages........and..

INDEX

INDEX